CULTURE SMART!
SWEDEN

Charlotte J. DeWitt

·K·U·P·E·R·A·R·D·

First published in Great Britain 2004
by Kuperard, an imprint of Bravo Ltd
59 Hutton Grove, London N12 8DS
Tel: +44 (0) 20 8446 2440   Fax: +44 (0) 20 8446 2441
www.culturesmartguides.com
Inquiries: sales@kuperard.co.uk

Culture Smart! is a registered trademark of Bravo Ltd

Distributed in the United States and Canada
by Random House Distribution Services
1745 Broadway, New York, NY 10019
Tel: +1 (212) 572-2844   Fax: +1 (212) 572-4961
Inquiries: csorders@randomhouse.com

Second printing (revised) 2006

Series Editor Geoffrey Chesler

ISBN-13: 978 1 85733 319 0
ISBN-10: 1 85733 319 5

British Library Cataloguing in Publication Data
A CIP catalogue entry for this book is available from the
British Library

Printed in Malaysia

This book is available for special discounts for bulk purchases for
sales promotions or premiums. Special editions, including
personalized covers, excerpts of existing books, and corporate
imprints, can be created in large quantities for special needs.

For more information in the U.S.A. write to Special
Markets/Premium Sales, 1745 Broadway, MD 6–2, New York,
NY 10019 or e-mail specialmarkets@randomhouse.com.

In the United Kingdom contact Kuperard publishers at the
above address.

Cover image: Gripsholm Castle, Mariefred.
Travel Ink/Leslie Garland

CultureSmart!Consulting and **Culture Smart!** guides have both
contributed to and featured regularly in the weekly travel program
"Fast Track" on BBC World TV.

About the Author

CHARLOTTE DEWITT is President of International Events, Ltd., and has produced nearly 150 festivals, events, and conferences. A native Bostonian and graduate of Drake University, U.S.A., she has lectured and consulted throughout North America, Europe, Australia, and Southeast Asia. She has written extensively on festivals and events as catalysts for cultural tourism and world understanding. Charlotte lived in Sweden for ten years and was President of The American Club of Sweden. She is First Vice President of the Federation of American Women's Clubs Overseas (FAWCO), which has special consultative status to the United Nations.

Other Books in the Series

- Culture Smart! Argentina
- Culture Smart! Australia
- Culture Smart! Belgium
- Culture Smart! Brazil
- Culture Smart! Britain
- Culture Smart! China
- Culture Smart! Costa Rica
- Culture Smart! Cuba
- Culture Smart! Czech Republic
- Culture Smart! Denmark
- Culture Smart! Finland
- Culture Smart! France
- Culture Smart! Germany
- Culture Smart! Greece
- Culture Smart! Hong Kong
- Culture Smart! Hungary
- Culture Smart! India
- Culture Smart! Ireland
- Culture Smart! Italy
- Culture Smart! Japan
- Culture Smart! Korea
- Culture Smart! Mexico
- Culture Smart! Morocco
- Culture Smart! Netherlands
- Culture Smart! New Zealand
- Culture Smart! Norway
- Culture Smart! Panama
- Culture Smart! Peru
- Culture Smart! Philippines
- Culture Smart! Poland
- Culture Smart! Portugal
- Culture Smart! Russia
- Culture Smart! Singapore
- Culture Smart! Spain
- Culture Smart! Switzerland
- Culture Smart! Thailand
- Culture Smart! Turkey
- Culture Smart! Ukraine
- Culture Smart! USA
- Culture Smart! Vietnam

Other titles are in preparation. For more information, contact: info@kuperard.co.uk

The publishers would like to thank **CultureSmart!**Consulting for its help in researching and developing the concept for this series.

CultureSmart!Consulting creates tailor-made seminars and consultancy programs to meet a wide range of corporate, public-sector, and individual needs. Whether delivering courses on multicultural team building in the U.S.A., preparing Chinese engineers for a posting in Europe, training call-center staff in India, or raising the awareness of police forces to the needs of diverse ethnic communities, we provide essential, practical, and powerful skills worldwide to an increasingly international workforce.

For details, visit www.culturesmartconsulting.com

contents

Map of Sweden	7
Introduction	8
Key Facts	10
Chapter 1: LAND AND PEOPLE	12
• Geographical Snapshot	13
• Climate	14
• The Swedish People: A Brief History	16
• The Swedes Today	25
• Sweden's Cities	26
• Government	28
• American Influence	30
• The Eurozone	31
Chapter 2: VALUES AND ATTITUDES	32
• *Lagom*: "Just Enough"	32
• *Jantelagen*: The Jante Law	33
• Fairness	35
• Equality	36
• Punctuality	37
• Patience	37
• Orderliness and Security	38
• Standing in Line	39
• The Swedish Model	40
• Royalty and the Class System	41
• Everyman's Right	42
• Svensson: A "Normal" Swede	43
• Marriage and Sexuality	43
• Consensus, Conformity, and Nonconfrontation	45
• Praise and Pride	46
• The Natural Swede	46
• The Work Ethic	47
• The Mobile Phone Culture	49
• The Homeland	49
• Attitudes Toward Outsiders	50
Chapter 3: CUSTOMS AND TRADITIONS	52
• The Swedish Year	52
• Religious Festivals	54
• Nonreligious Celebrations	59
• Other Festivals and Events	63

•	National Day	64
•	Award Ceremonies	64
•	Family Occasions	65
•	Religion	69

Chapter 4: MAKING FRIENDS — 70
•	Work and Social Life	71
•	Clothing	73
•	Greetings	74
•	Visitors Are Welcome	75
•	Joining Clubs	76
•	Invitations Home	78
•	Gift Giving	81
•	Emily Post Comes to Sweden	82

Chapter 5: THE SWEDES AT HOME — 84
•	Quality of Life	84
•	Living Conditions	85
•	Landscape and Architecture	87
•	Renting vs. Buying	87
•	Identity Cards and Residency	91
•	Family Life and Routines	92
•	Bounds and Boundaries	93
•	Sharing the Burden	94
•	Schools and Schooling	95
•	Changing Lifestyles	97

Chapter 6: TIME OUT — 98
•	Shopping	98
•	Banks and Currency Exchange	100
•	Restaurants, Food, and Drink	105
•	Leisure	109
•	Sports	110
•	High Culture	112
•	Popular Culture	113
•	The Great Outdoors	114

Chapter 7: GETTING AROUND — 116
•	Trains, Buses, and the Subway	116
•	Boats	118
•	Road Sense	119

contents

•	Local Transportation	123
•	Taxis	123
•	Where to Stay	124
•	Health and Security	127

Chapter 8: BUSINESS BRIEFING | | 130 |
•	Office Etiquette and Protocol	131
•	It's About Time!	133
•	The Coffee Culture	135
•	Business Entertaining	136
•	Mobile Phones	137
•	Management Styles	137
•	Women in Management	138
•	Leadership and Decision-Making	140
•	Presentation and Listening Styles	141
•	Negotiation Styles	142
•	Working in Sweden	143
•	Starting a Business in Sweden	144
•	Unions	147
•	Teamwork	148
•	Managing Disagreement	150

Chapter 9: COMMUNICATING | | 152 |
•	Language	152
•	TV and Radio	153
•	Making Contact	154
•	Telephones	155
•	Post	158
•	E-mail	160
•	Communication Styles	160
•	Cooperation	161
•	Honor	162
•	Conversation	162
•	Body Language	163
•	Conclusion	164

Further Reading | | **165** |
Index | | **166** |

Map of Sweden

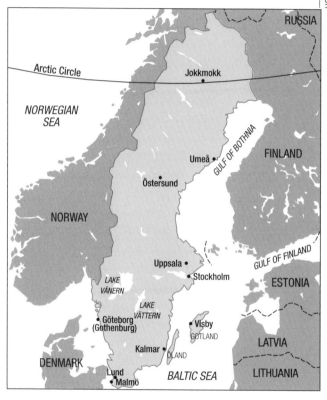

introduction

The Culture Smart! guides begin where most other travel books end. They emphasize people, not places. Written for the inquisitive traveler who wants more than research into hotels, sight-seeing, and transportation, they offer an insight into the human dimension of a country based on the values and attitudes of its people.

Sweden is an unspoiled paradise of vast, towering forests, beautiful mountains, and endless waterfront vistas dotted with thousands of islands. Its younger generation has readily embraced new ideas, but older Swedes retain a deep respect for their own cultural legacy.

If you are visiting Sweden for more than a few days, you will get much more out of your trip if you have a good background in the beliefs that make up the foundation of the Swedish way of life. *Culture Smart! Sweden* can help you get beyond the polite phase, so that you have a greater understanding of what is important to the Swedes and why they act the way they do. It considers the influence of Sweden's geography and history in shaping the national character. In addition to detailed information on deep-rooted Swedish values and attitudes, it gives a comprehensive overview of doing business in Sweden—essential information for anyone who needs to understand the unique way that Swedish businesses operate.

As for socializing, you will get an insider's perspective on visiting a Swedish home, as well as the qualities that Swedes most appreciate in a guest. With detailed chapters on the customs and traditions that form the cornerstones of life in Sweden, and information on how and where to meet and communicate with Swedes, this book is an indispensable guide to the "real" Sweden.

Sweden is a strikingly beautiful country with virtually no poverty and a profound reverence for a clean, tidy, and orderly natural environment. With a strong commitment to maintaining a safe and secure "home of the people," the Swedes are justifiably proud of creating what they consider to be a near-perfect society, with basic health, education, and social welfare benefits for all.

Culture Smart! Sweden provides a cultural roadmap to use in navigating the new social and professional situations you will encounter as a visitor, and will help you to build good business relationships and make firm friends with the welcoming and fair-minded people who live and work here.

Have a great trip!

Key Facts

Official Name	Kingdom of Sweden (*Kungariket Sverige*)	
Capital City	Stockholm	
Main Cities	Stockholm, Göteborg (Gothenburg), Malmö, Uppsala, Lund	
Area	174,000 sq. miles (450,660 sq. km)	Over 50% is forest; less than 10% is cultivated.
Climate	Temperate and cool	
Currency	Swedish krona (pl. kronor). In 2004, SEK 7.5 = 1 USD; SEK 13.5 = 1 GBP.	Sweden voted against joining the European Monetary Union in 2003.
Population	8.9 million	Average life expectancy is 77 for men, 82 for women.
Ethnic Makeup	89% Swedes; 11% others (c. 1 million first- and second-generation immigrants).	Sami (Lapps) are the indigenous people (approx. 20,000).
Family Makeup	The average number of children per family is 2.1.	
Language	Swedish. English has been taught in schools for the past 50 years.	Third language is often German or French.
Religion	Church and State were separated in 2000.	Evangelical Lutheran Church 82%; Roman Catholic 140,000; Pentecostal 100,000; Muslim 50,000; Jewish 16,000.

Government	Constitutional monarchy, parliamentary democracy. The monarch has no political power. The unicameral legislature, the *Riksdag*, has 349 members, and elections are every four years.	
Media	The Swedish Broadcasting Corporation runs two public-service TV channels, SVT1 and SVT2, as well as Radio Sweden. Three commercial channels: TV 3, TV 4, and Channel 5. Cable channels.	The largest national newspapers are *Dagens Nyheter* and *Svenska Dagbladet*. The west coast has *Göteborgs Posten*; the Malmö region has *Sydsvenska Dagbladet*. *Metro* and *Stockholm City* are free tabloids.
Media: English Language	Local TV channels often carry programming in English, as do the many English-language cable channels.	Radio Sweden and P6, Stockholm International carry programs in English. The *Stockholm Bulletin Magazine* is an English monthly.
Electricity	220 volts, 50 Hz.	Plugs are two-pronged. U.S. appliances need adapters for both current and plug.
Video/TV	PAL system	U.S. video systems are incompatible with PAL. Many people now buy dual-system VCRs.
Telephone	Sweden's country code is 46. To dial outside Sweden, dial 00 and then the country code.	To dial within Sweden using a mobile phone, dial 0 + the city code + the local number.

chapter one

LAND &
PEOPLE

A land of tall, blue-eyed blonds and short, dark Samis (Lapps), of ABBA and Absolut, Vikings and Volvos—Sweden is a study in contrasts. From a group of fierce, marauding warrior-tribes to a neutral, nonaligning nation of pacifists, the Swedish character has been molded by two major determinants: its landscape and its climate.

Nearly 9 million people inhabit this long, narrow country running 978 miles (1,574 km) from north of the Arctic Circle south to the sandy beaches of the province of Skåne. Nearly 90 percent of them live in the southern third of the country, which is so vast and underpopulated that if one were to apportion the land equally there would be one person per 12.5 acres (5 hectares). Too sparsely settled to be a major power-player in world politics, Sweden today has made its mark by taking the middle road of moderation and mediation. Yet prior to 1814, when permanent peace was established for the country, it was a great European power, its control encompassing the entire land around the Baltic Sea.

GEOGRAPHICAL SNAPSHOT

Sweden, together with Norway, constitutes the fingerlike Scandinavian peninsula pointing down to Denmark on the European continent. Until the opening of the Öresund Bridge connecting Denmark and Sweden in 2000, it was mainly accessible by air (in modern times) or by sea from continental Europe. This relative isolation has protected it from outside cultural and political influences throughout most of its history. Much of Sweden is bounded by water.

Sweden occupies 174,000 square miles (450,660 square kilometers). Over half of the country is forest, and less than 10 percent of the land is cultivated. A mountain ridge runs north and south along nearly the entire western border between Sweden and Norway. In the north and central regions of the country the forests of evergreens, pines, and spruce are so thick as to be

nearly impenetrable, forming the basis for
Sweden's rich forestry industry. If it were not for
the warming Gulf Stream off Norway's western
coast, much of the country would be
uninhabitable. Some 10,000 years ago, Sweden
was part of the polar ice cap. As this ice cap
melted and receded northward, it moved harshly
across the terrain, scraping the outcroppings of
rocks smooth, and leaving thousands of islands in
its wake. The archipelagoes off the east coast have
over 25,000 islands of varying size, ranging from
barren, uninhabited skerries to larger islands with
rocky coastlines that today provide nautical
Swedes with hours of enjoyment. Southern
Sweden is known for its beautiful sandy beaches.

Sweden's lake district, north and east of
Gothenburg, contains thousands of lakes. Vättern
and Vänern are two of the largest in Europe. The
Göta Canal, with its many locks, transects this
area, connecting Stockholm on the east coast with
Gothenburg on the west. Most of the population
of Sweden lives in the triangular area bounded by
Gothenburg, Stockholm, and Malmö.

CLIMATE

The Swedish climate is considered temperate and
cool, but in reality it, too, is a study in extremes.
Winters are long, dark, and cold, and seasonal

affective disorder (SAD), the "Lapp's disease," is so common that many Swedes have taken to combating this with exposure to special light panels, regular trips to suntanning salons, or winter travel to sunny climes. The average Swede is exceedingly well-traveled for this reason.

In the far north, the winter months can mean twenty-four hours of darkness, while the summer months offer the same amount of daylight.

Summer in Sweden is as close to heaven as most mortal Swedes get. The days are seemingly endless and, while not overly warm (63°F, 17°C), can reach 90°F (30°C), depending on location.

Average Temperatures		
	January	**July**
Malmö	31.6°F / -0.2°C	62.2°F/ 16.8°C
Stockholm	27.0°F/ -2.8°C	63.0°F/ 17.2°F
Kiruna	3.2°F / -16.0°C	55.0°F/ 12.8°C

Average Daylight		
	January	**July**
Malmö	7 hours	17 hours
Stockholm	6 hours	18 hours
Kiruna	0 hours	24 hours

Not unexpectedly, the Swedish personality reflects this extreme contrast: the Swedes in the summertime are gregarious, fun-loving extroverts, while in winter they become almost reclusive, using more candles per capita than any other people in the world.

Spring and fall are short, and many Swedes live by the motto *carpe diem*—if the day looks promising in terms of sun, they drop everything and seize the opportunity to go outdoors. This is often incomprehensible to those unfamiliar with the climate, particularly visiting business people.

THE SWEDISH PEOPLE: A BRIEF HISTORY
The Viking Age (800–1050 CE)

The evolution of the Swedish people from marauders to moderates is yet one more study in contrasts. In the ninth century Scandinavia—modern Denmark, Norway, and Sweden—was inhabited by a loose grouping of warlike Teutonic tribes known as the Vikings.

The Vikings raided most of Europe from the sea, gaining a fearsome reputation for brutality and destructiveness. The Danish and Norwegian Vikings took to the seas heading west and south, toward Ireland, Iceland, England, and France: the Swedish Vikings sailed mainly east, raiding and settling along the rivers of Russia, and founding the principality of Novgorod. Excellent shipbuilders, they developed easily portaged, flat-bottomed boats with long oars, enabling them to sail swiftly in and around the many islands and across lakes, and to carry the boats over dry land when necessary. Many of their conquests were due to this surprise factor.

Although in theory the boats would have allowed these farmers-turned-pirates to establish trade with other parts of the world, to begin with they found it more expedient to raid, plunder, and take slaves. Each warrior was entitled to his fair share of the spoils, a practice that foreshadowed the value system of Swedish citizens today.

From the Dark Ages to Enlightenment

How does a group of bloodthirsty warriors evolve into a nation known for its commitment to peace and moderation? First, the Viking conquests were not all purely destructive. In time, as merchants and settlers, they also interacted peaceably with other peoples, to their mutual benefit. In 1000 CE Sweden embraced Christianity and moved from a society of pagan kings living by plunder to a land of medieval kings supported by taxation. By 1210 an alliance was formed between Church and State, with implications that lasted until 2000, when the two were officially separated.

Concurrent with the acceptance of Christianity was the emergence of an aristocracy; rival dynasties competed for control of the Swedish kingdom, and a series of crusades incorporated western Finland. Dynastic struggles within all three Scandinavian countries led to the passing of the Swedish crown to Denmark, whose Queen Margareta became the most powerful ruler Scandinavia had ever known. Her political maneuverings resulted in the 1397 Union of Kalmar, which united Sweden, Norway, and Denmark. Thereafter Sweden was effectively ruled by a succession of regents.

The Union was plagued by conflict between the nobles and the Crown, as well as revolts by peasants and merchants against both, especially by the Swedes, who yearned for independence. The era came to an end in 1520 when the Danish King Christian II hosted a banquet in Stockholm as a peace overture and then, at its conclusion, locked the doors and beheaded over eighty Swedish noblemen whom he considered disloyal.

Unlike his father, brothers, and brother-in-law, Gustav Vasa survived the "Stockholm Bloodbath" to lead an uprising. He is said to have traveled by cross-country skis across Sweden to enlist the aid of those living in the province of Dalarna and in Norway. The reenactment of this is seen today with the famous *Vasaloppet*, or Vasa ski marathon.

The Vasa Era

Gustav Vasa was crowned King of Sweden on June 6, 1523, and the Kalmar Union came to an end. The Swedes today celebrate June 6 as their national day.

Under Gustav Vasa, Sweden was transformed from a federation of provinces into a nation based on a tiered class system of nobility, clergy, merchants, and peasants, all of which comprised the Parliament and endured until 1865. A powerful, enlightened, but ruthless ruler, he solved the country's financial crisis by transferring all Church property to the Crown in 1527, initiating the Swedish Reformation. Eventually Lutheranism came to replace Roman Catholicism as the State religion. In 1544 he established a hereditary monarchy. Lutheranism and the hereditary monarchy survive to this day.

Sweden as a Great Power

From 1611 to 1721 Sweden was the dominant power in northern Europe, controlling nearly the entire Baltic Sea after the Treaty of Roskilde in 1658 forced the Danes to relinquish the southern Swedish provinces of Skåne, Blekinge, and Halland. During this 110-year period the country was at war for seventy-two years, notably entering

Europe's Thirty Years War (1618–48) in 1631 against the Habsburg rulers of the Holy Roman Empire. The military brilliance of Gustav II Adolf (1611–32), "the Lion of the North," saved Protestantism in Germany. He made Stockholm Sweden's administrative capital.

His daughter Kristina (1633–54) became Sweden's first female monarch at the age of six. Her reluctance to marry caused the throne to be given to her cousin Karl Gustav. She abdicated and converted to Catholicism. As a result, the laws of succession were changed, barring women from the throne. They were repealed in 1979.

The Carolian Era

Karl X Gustav (1654–60) conquered Poland, invaded Denmark in a surprise move by leading his army across the frozen sea, and secured the southern Sweden provinces. Karl XI (1660–97) divided the land more evenly between the Crown, the nobility, and the peasants, while accruing absolute power. Karl XII (1697–1718) came to power as a teenager. His reign was controversial because he was always waging war. In 1718, he was shot in the head by his own men while besieging a fortress in Norway. By this time, he had lost almost all the territories Sweden had gained, with the exception of Finland and a small portion of Poland. Of the three treaties signed at this time, the most important was that signed in 1721 with Russia. It established certain present-day boundaries with Finland and Russia, and ended 150 years of nearly continuous war.

The Age of Liberty and the Gustavian Era

The eighteenth century was known as Sweden's "Age of Liberty." In 1719, a new constitution was adopted transferring political power from the king to parliament (the *Riksdag*), which was dominated by the nobles. This parliamentary rule lasted until around 1770. In 1772, the new king, Gustav III, staged a bloodless coup and claimed absolute power for himself.

Gustav III presided over a golden age in Swedish culture. He built the Royal Opera House and the Royal Dramatic Theater in Stockholm, and established the exquisite theater at Drottningholm Palace. In 1786, he founded the Swedish Academy, which today awards the Nobel Prize for Literature. However, he antagonized the nobility by attacking their privileges. In 1792, he was surrounded at a masked ball at the Opera and assassinated.

His son, Gustaf IV Adolf, abdicated and fled Sweden after losing Finland to Russia in the Napoleonic Wars of 1809. This cost Sweden one third of its land and marked the end of an era.

Karl Johan and the Era of Bourgeois Liberalism
The nineteenth century again saw power shifting
from the Crown to the people. Lacking an heir to
the throne, the nobles of the restored *Riksdag*
elected Napoleon's marshal, Count Jean-Baptiste
Bernadotte, Crown Prince of Sweden in 1810.
(The present royal family descends from the
Bernadottes.) A new constitution was adopted
that removed the absolute power of the monarch
and diminished the privileges of the aristocracy,
dividing power between the king, the
government, and parliament.

In 1812 Bernadotte allied Sweden with Russia
against France. In 1813 he defeated his former
commander, Napoleon, in the Battle of Leipzig,
and then attacked Denmark, forcing it to
sign the Treaty of Kiel in 1814, ceding
Norway to Sweden. The union
between Norway and Sweden lasted
nearly one hundred years, from 1814
to 1905. Bernadotte ruled Sweden from
1818 to 1844 as Karl XIV Johan.

One of the consequences of this near-century
of peace was that economic and agricultural
production did not keep up with the increase in
population. Between 1850 and 1930, famine and
economic hardship forced some 1.5 million
people to emigrate, mostly to the United States.
Some also wished for greater religious freedom.

From Agriculture to Industry

The nineteenth century saw the emergence of the middle class and strong religiosity characterized by abstinence from alcohol.

Sweden's Industrial Revolution began rather late, with unionization playing an increasingly powerful role, as witnessed by the first strike in 1879. By 1900 the population had grown to 5 million. Growing numbers moved to the towns to work in industry, since the land could no longer support them.

Free enterprise was established with the abolition of trade guilds and monopolies in 1846. Political reforms initiated by the serious-minded middle class included the creation of a bicameral legislature dominated by bureaucrats and farmers. In the late nineteenth century neutrality was adopted in foreign affairs, and in 1905 the union with Norway was dissolved. The year 1907 saw the adoption of proportional representation and universal suffrage.

These values are seen today in the makeup of the Social Democratic party, founded in 1889. It has been the dominant political party in Sweden since 1932, with the exception of six years in the 1970s and from 1991 to 1994, when a four-party nonsocialist government was in power with the chairman of the conservative Moderates, Carl Bildt, as prime minister. This consistency of government has contributed significantly to the country's stability over the past seventy years.

The Welfare State

In the 1920s an economic boom transformed the country from an agricultural to an industrial economy. Then came the Great Depression of the 1930s. The hardships suffered in Sweden were traumatic, and in its wake the Swedes determined to protect themselves against any recurrence of such poverty.

Having introduced a radical public works program to combat the slump, in 1936 the Social Democrats and the Agrarian Party developed the concept of a Welfare State that would guarantee unemployment benefits, paid holidays, childcare, and the right to good housing. The result of this "cradle to grave" safety net was that poverty more or less disappeared in Sweden.

Nonalignment

During the First and Second World Wars Sweden's policy of nonalignment and neutrality helped to preserve these gains, although at the moral price of not defending its neighbors Norway and Denmark, as well as not fighting Nazism. In 1940–43, under duress, neutral Sweden permitted limited transit of German forces through its territory. Covert assistance was given to the Allies.

The Postwar Years

From 1947 to 1969 Sweden's Social Democrat government perfected the comprehensive modern welfare state. In 1974 a constitutional change removed the remaining political powers of the monarch; in 1995 Sweden joined the European Union; and in 2000 the Lutheran Church and the State were formally separated after four hundred years. Two violent deaths—the assassination of Prime Minister Olof Palme in 1986 (which remains unsolved) and the murder of Foreign Minister Anna Lindh in 2003—marred this otherwise calm period, and have caused the Swedes to reassess their self-perception as a model, nonviolent society.

The effects of globalization and the rapid rise of the Internet and high-technology innovations have brought economic pressure to bear on Sweden, as well as opportunities. One of the challenges it faces today is to find a way to keep the positive features of its social democracy, while preventing a brain drain of youthful entrepreneurs and an exodus of labor-intensive businesses attracted to more supportive countries with lower taxation, social costs, and wages.

THE SWEDES TODAY

The most noticeable and possibly the most admirable change to occur in Sweden after the

Second World War has to do less with patriotism and political reform than with the cumulative effect of its reputation. Known as a fair, progressive, neutral country with an open-door policy, Sweden has attracted a continuous wave of immigrants over the past seventy-five years. Today, of the population of 8.9 million inhabitants, nearly one million are immigrants, about 50 percent of whom have Swedish citizenship. Many of these immigrants came as political refugees from southern and eastern Europe and the Middle East. By contrast, Sweden's indigenous people, the Sami (previously known as Lapps, a name they dislike), number only 20,000. The socioeconomic implications of integrating and providing services for such large numbers have resulted in more restrictive immigration policies in recent years.

Despite its small population, Sweden has made a big impact on the world in science, the arts, industry, technology, and sports. A Nobel Prize for an outstanding contribution in a particular field is the most prestigious award that can be won, and there can be few people who have not heard of Abba, Ingmar Bergman, or Björn Borg.

SWEDEN'S CITIES
The capital city of Stockholm is often called "the Venice of the North." Built on fourteen islands, it

looks out on another 25,000 islands in the Swedish archipelago. With a population of close to one million, it is the largest city in Sweden and lies in the lower third of the country. Slightly north of Stockholm is the university town of Uppsala (population 180,000) with its magnificent, eight-hundred-year-old cathedral.

Gothenburg (Göteborg, population 475,000), dominates Sweden's west coast and is a major gateway for commercial shipping and cruise ships. It lies in the center of a triangular area formed by Stockholm, Oslo, and Copenhagen, and is the worldwide export epicenter of carmakers Volvo and Saab. There is great rivalry between those living on "Sweden's front side" (*Sveriges framsida*) in predominantly blue-collar Gothenburg and the "*noll-åttas*" (0-8s), a derisive term for Stockholmers, derived from the city code of their telephone numbers.

At the southern tip of Sweden, Malmö (population 265,000), the third-largest city, is a charming combination of Danish-inspired architecture and Swedish history. Until the recent opening of the Öresund Bridge in 2000, people primarily crossed from Sweden to Denmark via ferry from neighboring Helsingborg. The university city of Lund (population 100,000) is only 19 miles (30 kilometers) away, and was at one time the religious capital of an extensive territory controlled by the Catholic Church that stretched from Iceland to Finland. Otherwise, much of urban Sweden comprises a few small cities and many smaller towns.

GOVERNMENT

The welfare state—described by Social Democrat Prime Minister Per Albin Hansson (1885–1946) as "a socially conscious society with financial security for all"—became the backbone of Sweden's model society, providing a broad safety net of social benefits, all funded by taxes. Hansson called this new society "the home of the people."

Political Parties

Although today there are seven major political parties, in practice two dominate almost all political activity: the Moderates, on the right, and the Social Democrats, on the left. Apart from the Left Party (the former Communist Party) on the far left, all other parties fall in between.

The political center point, equidistant from the Social Democrats and the Moderates, is the *Folkpartiet* (Liberal Party). The remaining parties cluster around this midpoint. Because Sweden is such a homogeneous society, there are no great differences between these parties.

THE MAIN PARTIES

Socialdemokraterna **(Social Democrats):** Left-wing. They believe the public sector should control social services, such as health, education, day care, workers' benefits. Pro-labor unions. Represent 90 percent of Sweden's blue-collar workers.

Moderaterna **(Moderates formerly called Conservatives):** Right-wing. Believe in lower taxes and a market economy based on free competition, including a private alternative to the state control of social services. Similar to America's Republican Party. Voter base is upper management and upper middle class.

Folkpartiet **(Liberals):** Exact center. Lie between the Moderates and Social Democrats and sway easily from one to the other. Platform: "social responsibility without socialism." Mainly educated middle- and lower-middle-class voters.

Kristdemokraterna **(Christian Democrats):** Originally from Småland. Represented interests of small, independent churches (non-Lutheran, e.g., Methodist, Baptist); now represent a more liberal constituency. Closer to the Moderates than the Folk Party. Strongly pro-EU and EMU. Voters: public-sector employees.

Vänsterpartiet **(Left Party):** Red. The former Communist Party; absorbed the left wing of the Social Democrats. Believes in a planned, state-owned economy.

Centern **(Center Party):** Originally known as the Agrarian Party, with provincially conservative values leaning toward the Social Democrats, but little intellectual substance. Close ties to rural Sweden.

Miljöpartiet **(Green Party):** Green. Environmental issues are focal point. Attracts young people.

AMERICAN INFLUENCE

Sweden enjoys a paradoxical relationship with America. In the mid 1800s and early 1900s, nearly a million Swedes emigrated to the United States, largely as a result of crop failure and famine in the 1850s, but also because of a desire for more religious freedom and to avoid being drafted into military service, conscription having been introduced in 1901. By 1930, this number had increased to 1.5 million.

Most of these emigrants were farmers who settled in the Midwestern region, particularly Minnesota, where land was plentiful and fertile. However, by 1905 upward of 20 percent of them had returned to Sweden. According to the records of the American Club of Sweden, founded in 1905 as the Swedish-American Society of Stockholm, these repatriated Swedes brought with them a sense of openness, optimism, and helpfulness, as well as new business ideas that they had acquired in the U.S.A. The American Women's Club of Sweden, founded in 1911, also documents an increasing interaction between America and Sweden, as returning businessmen brought back American wives along with new business ideas.

Today, many young Swedes go to the U.S.A. to work as au pairs or to study, and, with the globalization of business, others are sent there by their companies to work. The IT boom and

Sweden's reputation as the Silicon Valley of Europe, as well as the well-known American spirit of entrepreneurship, further enhance this positive image of cooperation between the two countries.

Although American logos and the English language pervade Sweden, there is a subtle yet persistent resistance by the Swedes to the threat, real or implied, of American homogenization of their culture. The political position of the U.S.A. with regard to Iraq in 2003–04 marred this relationship even further.

THE EUROZONE

If Swedes are wary of the Americanization of their culture, they are equally fearful of losing their identity within the European Union. In 1995, the country voted by a narrow margin to join the EU, but in 2003 it rejected entry into the European Monetary Union on the grounds that Sweden would lose its ability to react to global economic changes by tying its currency to the Euro and the economic fluctuations of the other EU countries. The EMU issue will not come up for reconsideration in Sweden before 2010.

chapter two

VALUES & ATTITUDES

Sweden's extremes in geography, climate, and history have given rise to a national personality that reveres homogeneity, honesty, self-sufficiency, and earnest, self-effacing sincerity, and avoids conspicuousness and confrontation. The end result is a person who is modest, reserved, and romantically nationalistic. Underneath those layers, you will find a dry sense of humor, a fervent adoration of nature, and a great love of home and family.

The ideal world, seen through the eyes of a Swede, would be founded on the principles of equality and fairness. There are two aspects of these values that give them a particularly Swedish slant: *lagom* and *Jantelagen*.

LAGOM: "JUST ENOUGH"

The Swedish word *lagom* expresses a concept that dates back to the Vikings. It has no equivalent in English, but is loosely translated as "just enough." As the story goes, the Vikings celebrated a victory by drinking a toast from a horn or communal bowl filled with mead, an alcoholic drink made of fermented honey and water. As the bowl passed from one set of hands to the next, "around the team" (*laget om),* each man was to drink just enough (*lagom*) to quench his thirst, but not so much as to deprive the remaining guests of their fair share. It was an intuitive sense of what was "just enough," not only for oneself, but also for each of the remaining celebrants, and it is a value that is strongly ingrained in the personality of the Swedes to this day.

It is easy to see *lagom* at work around a dinner table, but the principle also operates in business situations and in the social welfare system, where each person is given "just enough" to meet his basic living needs, but not too much. Those who are perceived to have more than their share are taxed at progressively higher rates in order to provide for those who do not.

JANTELAGEN: THE JANTE LAW

Every culture is underpinned by a set of social principles governing the day-to-day behavior of people. In his novel *A Fugitive Crosses His Tracks* the early twentieth-century Danish-Norwegian author Aksel Sandemose listed ten rigid laws designed to keep people in their psychological places in the imaginary Nordic village of "Jante."

The first of these was "thou shalt not believe thou *art* something." The remaining laws admonished the reader not to think of himself as wiser, better, more knowledgeable, or more important than anyone else. If that were not depressing enough, he should not *ever* believe that he would amount to anything, or think that anyone cared about him. So profound an effect did this novel have on its readers that the contemporary Swedish values of extreme modesty, humility, and self-restraint are said to derive directly from the Jante Law.

In short, perfectly normal, successful Swedes go to great pains to appear to be no better than anyone else because this would not be fair or equitable. It extends to the way people dress (no bright colors or flashy jewels), their cars (no identifying indicia on top-of-the-line models), their demeanor in public (no loud laughter), and their inability to accept compliments gracefully. The dire consequence of standing out is to incur the populist wrath known as "the royal Swedish envy" ("*den kungliga svenska avundsjukan*"), where one's fate, like that of the proverbial Australian "tall poppy," could be the public humiliation of being cut down to size.

In the twenty-first century, the unfortunate side effect of this ethos has been to discourage young Swedes from becoming entrepreneurs. The Jante Law has created a society that tends not to cross the psychological line to praise, support, or otherwise encourage the entrepreneur, the artist, or the inventor—because they are different and that would upset the norm—and a school system that does not encourage competitiveness and individual achievement.

By comparison, Americans demonstrate its antithesis: they are extremely self-confident, proud of their successes, and do not hesitate to show it. Success in America usually brings money, which in the land of conspicuous consumption leads to excessive spending, demonstrating how successful you were to earn the money.

In recent years, due to the IT revolution and increased exposure to American values among the younger generation, a new breed of Swede has emerged that rejects the Jante Law.

FAIRNESS

As an extension of the concept of *lagom*, fairness, in the Swedish context, means that everyone has just enough, and that all share equally. If some have more than others, they give more via taxes so that those less fortunate or less successful have more. That is fair.

The American interpretation of fairness is

slightly different. Everybody should have the opportunity to get his or her share. Depending on how people exercise that opportunity, some people will get larger shares. This, too, is seen as fair, since they may have worked harder or had a better business idea than other people.

EQUALITY

Gender discrimination is illegal in Sweden, but the "glass ceiling" still exists. State-subsidized childcare (and elder care) makes it possible for the mother of small children (or the nurturer) to return to work without losing most of her paycheck to day-care workers. Over 80 percent of Swedish women work outside the home, and some 48 percent of the labor force are female; however, women on the whole still earn less than men. Philosophically, Swedish society encourages all people to be self-supporting. Self-sufficiency is highly valued. From a taxation standpoint, there is no advantage to being married, as both partners are taxed and must file their returns separately.

In terms of parenting, each parent shares the responsibility, and it is not uncommon to see two fathers pushing baby carriages together. Approximately 80 percent of the nonworking parent's wages are covered during the first twelve to eighteen months of the child's life, and this time period may be shared in any proportion between the two parents. In practice, it is usually the mother who stays at home.

PUNCTUALITY

The importance of punctuality in Sweden is paramount: not five minutes early and not five minutes late, but exactly and precisely on time. In Sweden, it is a social art form elevated to the highest stature. People will walk around the block rather than be early.

In a business context, your punctuality is an acknowledgment that everyone's time is equally important, and that you are not attempting some sort of power play or grand entrance by being late. Being late draws attention to yourself, which, as we have seen, is not a positive quality, and it disrupts the meeting already in progress—it will have started on time, without you.

PATIENCE

In Sweden patience is both a virtue and a necessity, since all are equal and no one is entitled to any special treatment. Patience fits in well with the Swedish respect for nonconfrontation and calmness, and is an essential part of keeping things running smoothly.

Restaurants require patience. Your needs are no greater than those of the other diners, or of the waiter, who is paid by the hour and whose tip is included in your bill. Patience is also required in meetings, where each person is encouraged to give his point of view and no one interrupts until the speaker is finished. This will be addressed further in the business chapter.

Also, keep in mind the difficulty of thinking and speaking in a foreign language. Pauses or slowness require patience when someone is struggling to express himself in your language, not his own. The Swedes are economical conversationalists, and they will not talk unnecessarily or think out loud the way that Americans do. Once committed verbally, however, the Swede sets great store on keeping his word. Verbal agreements are considered binding.

ORDERLINESS AND SECURITY

There is in Sweden a time and a season, or a time and a place, for everything. A structured and orderly way of life is the natural outcome of patience. To an outsider, the Swedes may appear to be compulsively orderly, but this gives them a sense of security.

Consensus is the process that ensures a feeling of safety—the idea that if all have participated in the decision-making process there will be no unexpected surprises, and the comfort level of conformity will be maintained.

The need for security transfers itself to industry, in the production of what are regarded as two of the safest automobiles in the world—Saab and Volvo—as well as the invention of the safety match and safety belts for cars. And, of course, the social safety net of the "Swedish Model" provides government-guaranteed security in the form of pensions, health care, day care, workers' rights, and education.

STANDING IN LINE

The Swedes have developed a queuing system of taking a numbered ticket, called a *nummerlapp*, dispensed from a machine.

Surviving the Line

As a rule of thumb, head for the little dispensing machine the minute you enter the room. Some machines have more than one choice, always written in Swedish, of course. When in doubt, take one of each. You will be a hero when you give away the unused low-number slip to a frustrated customer.

THE SWEDISH MODEL

While Sweden had actively recruited a new royal family in 1810, it was the institution of monarchy, in the opinion of many, that had kept the nation at war for so many centuries and rewarded the nobility while the common people suffered. Thus, even though the hundred years of peace actually created a state of poverty in the mid 1800s—as a result of the disproportionate growth of the population relative to the resources of the country—the people blamed the Crown. They increasingly transferred power and loyalty away from the throne, and invested it in a democracy based on social welfare reform.

Today's "cradle to grave" system of benefits delivers that most cherished of Swedish states of mind, security. Many may complain of high taxes (the highest "value-added tax," or sales tax, in the world, at 25 percent), but all will agree that people have a universal and fundamental right to the benefits of this social safety net: health, education, day care, and a broad range of workers' rights and compensation.

Believing that theirs is the model society, the "third way" between capitalism and communism, the Swedes naturally assume a somewhat superior attitude toward countries not following this model. To outsiders, they can sometimes appear to be complacent and unmotivated. The high taxation required to support such a social safety net is levied progressively, with the result being that even after a significant promotion at work, one may not see an appreciable increase in take-home pay. This is a disincentive to hard work. The protection offered by Sweden's strong labor laws makes it virtually impossible to fire an employee, if for no other reason than the expense it entails. Therefore, employees do not fear for job security, no matter how mediocre their performance.

ROYALTY AND THE CLASS SYSTEM

Sweden's royal family today is well-liked and respected, but has no real power. King Carl XVI Gustaf and his beautiful wife, Queen Silvia, preside at official state functions and serve in a public relations capacity to represent the country. A 1979 revision to the constitution now allows females to accede to the throne, thus clearing the way for Crown Princess Victoria eventually to become the first ruling Queen since Queen Kristina abdicated in 1654. Prince Carl Philip and Princess Madeleine, the other two royal siblings, are also popular with Swedes.

The Swedish nobility still exists, although today it consists of only 608 families totaling 26,000 members out of a population of almost nine million. Although the King's right to grant noble status ended with constitutional reform in 1975, there is still a certain respect for the nobility, and many individuals from noble families over the years have been prominent political figures with a keen sense of duty to their country.

The Noble Crest

Members of the nobility often wear a gold signet ring with the family crest engraved on it. Shields bearing the noble crests are on display at the Church of the Nobility (*Riddarkyrkan*) and in the Swedish House of Nobility (*Riddarhuset*).

Since the labor reforms of the 1930s and the subsequent strengthening of social welfare benefits, the middle class has become the dominant class in Sweden. All people are considered roughly equal. In theory, status ceases to be important, but in fact "the royal Swedish envy" would indicate otherwise. The outward trappings of status, however, are downplayed, as it is not acceptable to flaunt wealth.

EVERYMAN'S RIGHT

A unique aspect of the belief that "every man is equal" is the Swedish belief in equal access to private lands. *Allemansrätten,* or "every man's right," allows the free and open enjoyment of all land, even private property, as long as it does not disturb the owner or result in any destruction of the property. Sailors may anchor and use beaches, hikers may hike, campers may camp one night as long as everything is left neat and tidy upon departure.

SVENSSON: A "NORMAL" SWEDE

America has its average father and husband immortalized in "Ozzie and Harriet." Sweden has Svensson, the "normal" Swede who lives in the suburbs with his wife and their 2.1 kids, a Volvo station wagon, and a dog. All in all, he is a self-effacing, humble person not given to a lot of idle talk, and fairly direct and unadorned in his speech when he does talk. His sense of humor can be dry and subtle, and he publicly exhibits no great swings of emotion. In former times, to be described as "just a normal Swede" would have been taken as a compliment. Today this phrase might be used with irony, but self-sufficiency and self-restraint are still encouraged.

MARRIAGE AND SEXUALITY

Ever the realists, the Swedes are very matter-of-fact about marriage and sexuality. It is common for couples to live together in an unmarried state (*samboende,* or *sambo* for short) or to be committed to each other, but live apart (*särbo*). Today, neither religion nor pregnancy is a compelling reason to marry. It is not unusual for a couple to decide to marry several years down the line, with their children serving as ring bearers and flower girls. Homosexual marriages have been legal since 1995.

Those living together but unmarried are protected by law (*Sambolagen*) upon the dissolution of their relationship. Unless there is a written pre-cohabitation agreement, each partner is entitled to exactly half of all the couple's assets.

Sweden has a famously liberal attitude toward sexuality; a recent consequence of this is that Swedish teenagers now bring a boyfriend or girlfriend home for the night. The teens defend this by saying it is preferable to having sexual encounters in parked cars; the parents, although fairly uncomfortable, at least initially, with this overt expression of sexual activity by their children, usually come to allow it. One farsighted mother decided that it was her duty to bring the romantic couple breakfast in bed the next morning. It quickly put a stop to the visits.

CONSENSUS, CONFORMITY, AND NONCONFRONTATION

The Swedes value homogeneity and horizontal rather than hierarchal decision-making. They have a strong need to avoid confrontation, matched by an equally strong desire to reach a decision by consensus. Thus most business meetings strive to achieve a decision palatable to all through discussion and compromise, rather than voting along black and white lines.

When participating in a Swedish meeting, it is wise to predetermine how the decision will be reached. A high-level diplomat at the U.S. Embassy in Stockholm coined the term "intuitive consensus" to describe the ability of Swedish participants to leave a meeting tacitly understanding that a decision had been arrived at, while the Americans had missed the cues.

The Swedes use social pressure to enforce conformity. This can be seen early in life in day-care centers, where a misbehaving or unruly child in a play group is ignored or asked to go leave the room. On an adult level, residents of an apartment building, if they are frustrated in their attempts to live harmoniously with a neighbor, may behave as if this person did not exist.

In a business context, while it is not difficult to get an initial meeting or contact with a fairly senior person, if that person is not interested in your proposal, there may not be a direct rejection (because that would require confrontation and high emotion). The proposal would simply wither on the vine. The business equivalent of being cold-shouldered is that e-mails, faxes, and written correspondence will not be responded to, phone calls may not be put through or returned, and future appointments may be cancelled and not rescheduled, or languish awaiting confirmation of a date that, of course, never comes.

By the same token, a Swede puts great value in a verbal agreement, and once having given approval, considers himself honor-bound to uphold it. The judicial system supports this.

PRAISE AND PRIDE

While individual Swedes often find it difficult to accept praise, they will point with pride to famous Swedes, and they feel a certain satisfaction that they are living in a model society surrounded by an ecologically pure environment.

THE NATURAL SWEDE

The Swede's reverence for nature extends into every aspect of life. Fiercely proud and protective of their country's pristine waters, unpolluted air, beautiful forests, and vast mountain ranges, they worship nature in all its glory and work hard to keep it that way through vigorous recycling and environmentally friendly behavior. It is, in many respects, their religion.

In their choice of materials for clothing, gift-wrap, or interior design, the natural prevails: cotton, linen, or wool fibers; simple bows and ribbons on plain paper; colors that exist in a natural state, such as berry red or dark evergreen. Christmas tree ornaments are made of straw and wood. Makeup for women is unobtrusive; bright red nail polish may raise an eyebrow.

THE WORK ETHIC

To a person coming from a more robustly capitalist country, the Swedish attitude toward work may be difficult to understand. While many other cultures are business-driven and profit-motivated, the Swedes greatly value their private time with their friends and family, and draw a strict line between business and pleasure.

Because they believe there is more to life than work, the idea of a lifestyle driven by work is totally abhorrent to Swedes. Rather than being praised, the workaholic is treated with suspicion: perhaps he is not using his time efficiently if he needs to work so many more hours than he is paid for, or possibly his personal life is not fulfilling. His efforts to shine may also make his colleagues look bad by comparison. The Jante Law condemned the workaholic, since he or she was forbidden to stand out from the crowd.

Although Lutheranism says hard work builds character and is socially redeeming, the notion of *lagom* dictates that a man should work "just enough" and be paid "just enough." Finally, even if a man could be convinced to work overtime, Sweden's progressive taxation would eat away any additional monies gained in this way. All one needs in terms of the basics is already provided for by the state.

This attitude toward work defeats the very spirit of enterprise, which entails risk-taking, dedication, and long hours of labor. Ironically, the national "Entrepreneur of the Year" award is frequently given to a company executive, rather than an owner or investor. Outside Sweden, entrepreneurs are rarely employees.

The high-tech revolution, characterized by near-instantaneous communication with colleagues abroad, has begun to chip away at the old Swedish work ethic, especially within the younger generation so inspired by California's Silicon Valley and the dot com industry. The brain drain to more profit-driven countries with limitless opportunities and lower taxes is having an impact on Sweden.

THE MOBILE PHONE CULTURE

It would be hard to find a culture where mobile (cellular) telephones are more pervasive. They are turned on almost twenty-four hours a day, even in business meetings, and no self-respecting Swede would allow himself to be inaccessible for any length of time unless, of course, his battery ran out. Rather than resenting the intrusion into their lifestyles, most Swedes are annoyed if they cannot be reached virtually all the time. Parents may also control their children's use of mobile phones by programing them to receive messages, but only to call home.

THE HOMELAND

Swedish nationalism is not about flag-waving, since Sweden has had a long history of neutrality and nonalignment, but rather is a romanticized love affair with the natural, unspoiled beauty of the country. There is something special about unspoiled landscapes, highways without billboards, water without pollution, mountain vistas, and ocean views. All Swedes carry this postcard-perfect memory with them no matter where in the world they go.

However, the older Swede is pragmatic when it comes to the long winter season. In recent years, warm-weather winter destinations such as Florida, California, Spain, and Portugal have attracted those trying to escape the extremes of winter, returning to the homeland only when the land has thawed.

ATTITUDES TOWARD OUTSIDERS

Sweden's liberal immigration policy of former years has resulted in a population mix that is approximately 11 percent non-Swedish and has created an ambivalence toward outsiders. On the one hand, immigrant labor helped equalize the labor shortage caused by emigration to America. On the other, the result has been higher social costs and a Sweden that visually does not resemble its old self. The impact of American culture has also caused many Swedes to fear losing their language to English, and their calm, Nordic way of life to the frenzy of the fast lane.

The emergence of Sweden as a leader in new growth areas such as pharmaceuticals, information technology, and telecommunications has also contributed to this ambivalence, as major multinationals send expatriates to start up or firm up their operations in Sweden, and Swedish-owned international companies recruit external competence to guide them into a competitive stance in the global arena.

Up to a point, outsiders are tolerated. Tourists are warmly welcomed (since they bring money into the country rather than out), and all Swedes are unusually helpful and open toward them. Expatriates posted to Sweden for business reasons are welcomed as long as the Swedes can see a beginning and an end to the assignment. Rarely is an American businessman assigned to Sweden expected to learn the language.

Sweden traditionally has shown great compassion toward the underprivileged, especially those from war-torn or Third World countries. It is very generous in providing the mechanisms, such as free language and lifestyle classes, to enable immigrants to assimilate into the culture. These people are the ones who often will fill low-paying, low-status jobs.

Because of relatively high unemployment (the official rate is 5.1 percent, but this does not take into account those who are enrolled in retraining programs and those not listed at all), the Swedes are naturally protective of the jobs that do exist and are not receptive to outsiders, whatever their qualifications, who may take work away from them. This protective attitude will never manifest itself overtly. The end result, however, is the same: on a permanent basis, Sweden is for Swedes. American or English-speaking temporary visitors, though, are warmly welcomed.

CUSTOMS & TRADITIONS

While life in some countries is ordered by the calendar, in Sweden it revolves around the sun. If you can imagine a country so dark in the wintertime that even its southernmost provinces have only a few hours of dim light each day, then you will have some idea of the utter joy that erupts once the sun returns. Swedish holiday customs and traditions follow this cycle.

THE SWEDISH YEAR

There are twelve legal holidays—so-called "red days"—in Sweden. Most are religious-based. The "red day" holidays appear in bold type opposite.

DATE	SWEDISH HOLIDAY	ENGLISH NAME
January 1	*Nyårsdagen*	New Year
January 6	*Trettondedag Jul*	Epiphany
January 13	*Tjugondedag Knut*	Knut Hilarymas
February/March	*Fastlag (Fettisdag)*	Lent (Shrove Tuesday)
March 25	*Marie Bebådelsedag*	Annunciation
March/April	*Långfredagen*	Good Friday ("Long" Friday)
March/April	*Påsk*	Easter
March/April	*Annandag Påsk*	Easter Monday ("Another" Easter Day)
April 30	*Valborgsmässoafton*	Walpurgis Night
May 1	*Första Maj*	May Day
Middle/end of May	*Kristi Himmelsfärdsdag*	Ascension Day
Last Sunday in May	*Mors dag*	Mother's Day
May/June	*Pingst*	Whitsun
June 6	*Sveriges nationaldag*	Sweden's National Day
End of June	*Midsommar*	Midsummer
October/November	*Alla Helgons dag*	All Saints' Day
November 11	*Mårtensgås*	St. Martin's Day
Second Sunday in Nov.	*Fars dag*	Father's Day
4th Sunday before Christmas	*Advent*	Advent
December 10	*Nobeldagen*	Nobel Day
December 13	*Luciadagen*	Lucia
December 24	*Julafton*	Christmas Eve
December 25	**Jul**	Christmas
December 26	**Annandag Jul**	Christmas Monday
December 31	*Nyårsafton*	New Year's Eve

RELIGIOUS FESTIVALS

Advent

On the four Sundays preceding Christmas, the
Swedes light Advent candles, one candle being
added each week. There are many colorful
Christmas markets in the town squares during
Advent. There are also festive open-house parties
where hot mulled wine (*glögg*) and gingersnap
cookies (*pepparkakor*) are served.

Lucia

It is ironic that predominantly Lutheran Sweden
begins its Christmas season at the very darkest
time of the year with the celebration of an Italian
Catholic saint. On the morning of December 13,
in households all over Sweden, young girls dress
up in long white cotton nightgowns with scarlet
ribbons tied around their waists. The part of
Lucia is usually played by the youngest girl, who
wears a crown or a wreath encircled with candles.
Boys participate as "star boys," wearing long,
white nightshirts and tall, conical hats. With a
breakfast tray of freshly baked saffron buns
shaped like cats (*Lussekatt*),
the children sing "Santa
Lucia" to wake their
parents. Throughout the day in
schools, offices, and other public places
this ritual is reenacted, sometimes with a

humorous slant, particularly if there are no females present to play Lucia. Many communities also elect an official Lucia, who visits hospitals with her attendants. There is also an annual Swedish Lucia contest in which the winner is crowned in a ceremony at the Skansen open-air museum in Stockholm.

Christmas (*Jul*)

Christmas arrives on December 24. Families exchange presents, called *julklapp* (Christmas "knocks"), and eat dinner on Christmas Eve. Every Swedish home has a straw goat (*julbock*), a symbol of the devil that dates back to the Middle Ages. Watching Donald Duck, or *Kalle Anka*, on TV on December 24 is now as much a Christmas tradition as the arrival of the Swedish version of Santa Claus, the *tomte*, a gnome-like, wizened old man with a long white beard, who conveniently waits until the cartoon finishes before delivering the presents. In some families, each present is accompanied by a rhyme or riddle, which must be solved before the gift can be opened.

The traditional Christmas dinner follows: a buffet table (*smörgåsbord*) groaning with pickled herring (*sill*), smoked salmon, liver pâté, smoked sausages, and cold spare ribs; crisp, unleavened bread and an array of cheeses; plus the hot dishes of miniature hotdogs, meatballs, Jansson's Temptation (a gratin casserole of potatoes and anchovies), red cabbage spiced with cloves, and the *pièce de résistance*, the Christmas ham. Dessert may simply be a bowl of fresh fruit.

That evening, the truly gastronomically courageous proceed onward to dried ling or sathe (*lutfisk*), a type of cod that has been soaked, softened, and boiled to either a fluffy or a jellylike consistency. It is served smothered in melted butter and/or a cream sauce. Dessert is often boiled rice porridge with one almond lurking within. The finder of the almond will be the next to marry—or must recite a poem.

Christmas Day itself begins with a very early morning church service. It is a family day, spent with jigsaw puzzles, board games, books, and long walks out of doors. There is, of course, another Christmas dinner, this time possibly goose. In recent years, turkey has become popular.

Annandag Jul

December 26 is also a legal holiday. It is worth noting that, as with the summer solstice, very little work gets done in Sweden during this winter solstice period between December 13 and mid-January, as most people are celebrating. Many also travel abroad in search of the sun.

Epiphany (*Trettondedag Jul*)

The holy day of Epiphany (*trettondedag jul,* literally translated as "thirteenth day Christmas"), on January 6, is a legal holiday, and in many countries marks the end of the long Christmas holiday period. Swedes, however, prolong the festivities another week, until January 13, when the children of the family and their friends gather together to strip the tree of its ornaments, play games, eat, drink, and make merry. This occasion is known as *Tjugondedag Knut*, meaning the twentieth day after Christmas, which is observed on the "name day" of Knut, a man's name. In Sweden, each day of the year has a first name associated with it. Out goes the tree, and the Christmas season is officially over.

Easter (*Påsk*)

The pagan and the sacred are intermingled at Easter. Little girls tie kerchiefs over their heads, wear their mothers' long skirts, and go door-to-door as colorful witches begging for sweets. Swedish folklore has it that at Easter the witches flew to visit the devil on Blue Mountain (*Blåkulla*) and must be kept from returning. The treats are said to appease them. In some communities, bonfires are symbolically lit on the Saturday before Easter to keep the witches at bay. Everyone loves painting Easter eggs.

The days, while still cold, are increasingly sunny. Birch twigs are brought indoors, immersed in water, and decorated with chicken feathers dyed bright shades of yellow, orange, turquoise, and purple. As the season advances toward the vernal equinox, the buds burst into tender green leaves foretelling the arrival of spring.

With less than 5 percent of the people attending church regularly, the four days off at Easter represent a welcome opportunity to squeeze in one last ski trip, do some spring cleaning, or start preparing the boat for the water.

The traditional Easter foods include salmon for Good Friday (called "Long" Friday by Swedes), eggs on Saturday, and, more recently, an Easter Sunday dinner of leg of lamb, made possible only by modern refrigeration and transportation, since Swedish lambing occurs much later in the season. Alternately, there is the Easter ham. During Lent, sweet buns filled with marzipan and topped with whipped cream (*semla*) are a popular treat.

Ascension Day (*Kristi Himmelsfärdsdag*)
This falls five and a half weeks after Easter, usually in May. Because it is always on a Thursday, Swedes enjoy a long weekend.

Whitsunday and Whitmonday (*Pingstdagen* and *Annandag Pingst*)

These legal holidays are a week and a half after Ascension Day, and create another three-day weekend.

All Saints' Day (*Alla Helgons dag*)

All Saints' Day is celebrated on the first Saturday after October 30. Families place wreaths and special, long-burning candles on the graves of their departed loved ones. For those living a great distance from their family gravesites, communal remembrance areas exist at most cemeteries.

NONRELIGIOUS CELEBRATIONS
New Year's (*Nyårsafton*)

New Year's Eve is a time for neighborhood fireworks at midnight. In cities, people throng the streets no matter how cold the weather. While the younger set usually goes out to restaurants and discothèques, older people more often entertain quietly but lavishly in their homes, serving champagne and lobster flown in from Canada. Upon a hilltop at the outdoor museum Skansen in Stockholm, just before midnight, a prominent Swede recites a Swedish translation of the poem "Ring out, Wild Bells" by Alfred, Lord Tennyson. On the stroke of twelve, all the church bells throughout the city ring in the New Year. Fireworks follow. The event is broadcast nationally on both television and radio.

The first day of January is a legal holiday. Often there are excellent concerts in the churches.

Walpurgis Night (*Valborgsmässoafton*)

April 30, also the birthday of the present monarch, King Carl XVI Gustaf, is the eve of the feast of St. Walburga, when university students and former students gather in front of bonfires all over Sweden to sing songs welcoming spring. They wear their white student caps with black visors. More often than not, it is raining, sleeting, or otherwise miserable weather, but the tradition is as sturdy as the singers.

May Day

May 1 is Labor Day throughout much of Europe. Today, the May Day parade is a calm, ceremonial occasion. Representatives and members of most of the political parties and labor unions gather under their respective banners to march through the streets and listen to speeches in a nearby park. It is a legal holiday.

Midsummer

Midsummer's Eve is celebrated on the Friday of the weekend closest to June 24. This is a time of twenty-four-hour sunlight in the far north, and a few hours of velvety purple at night in the south. Boats are in the water, the summerhouse is opened up, and nothing is more lovely on the face of the earth. Early in the day, wildflowers are gathered and woven into wreaths to be hung from the maypole. All gather around to sing traditional songs and dance, often to the accompaniment of an accordion and a fiddle. A feast of pickled herring, crispbread, and new potatoes follows, interspersed with much singing and toasting with *snaps* (schnapps), a potent, if flavored, relative of vodka, washed down with a beer chaser. Dessert is fresh strawberries and cream or ice cream. According to folklore, a maiden who places seven different wildflowers under her pillow before falling asleep will dream of her future husband.

Crayfish in August

August 8 is traditionally the time for crayfish parties. These miniature versions of a lobster are cooked in salted water and fresh dill, and eating them means much slurping and sucking to remove the crayfish meat from the bright red shells. This, in turn, necessitates a round of *snaps*, drinking songs, and beer chasers. People wear conical (and comical) party hats and paper bibs, and paper lanterns shaped like smiling full moons are strung from the trees. It is one of the few times

you will see a Swede use his fingers to eat food . . .
or voluntarily look silly.

Fermented Herring (*Surströmming*)
The eating of fermented herring is an acquired
skill. Even among Swedes it is a minority activity,
once confined to northern Sweden. Participants
require copious quantities of *snaps*, as well as
edible aids such as flat bread and goat's cheese, to
survive the experience. These parties are usually
held in mid-August, when the one-year
fermentation process has caused the tin container
to bulge and threaten to explode. Opening the
container, therefore, is an art in itself. Then eat the
whole fish quickly and all at once, preferably
following it immediately with a slice of bread.
Don't prolong the agony by taking small bites.
Remember to resume breathing.

Goose in November: St. Martin's Day
This feast day on November 11 originally
celebrated the memory of St. Martin of Tours,
but eventually came to honor Martin Luther.
It is not a legal holiday. Roast goose
is typically served, preceded by a
bowl of dark soup made from
goose-blood and spices (to which
consommé is an acceptable
alternative!).

OTHER FESTIVALS AND EVENTS

There are many nonreligious events throughout the year: music festivals, such as those during the summer at the restored eighteenth-century Drottningholm Court Theater or at Ulriksdal Castle; "pop" festivals, such as the Hultsfred Rock Festival in June; and the Stockholm International Jazz & Blues Festival in late July.

Carnival revelry takes place in the university town of Lund each spring, and at the Royal Technical School (KTH or *Kungliga Tekniska Högskolan*) in Stockholm every three years in May. The Gay Pride Parade in Stockholm in August takes carnival to a new level.

Also in August are the Gothenburg Party (*Göteborgs Kalaset*), the Malmö Festival, and the Medieval Festival Week within the ancient walled city of Visby on the island of Gotland.

In February, check out the town of Jokkmokk's Great Sami Winter Fair, a 400-year-old annual crafts market of Sami handicrafts and reindeer revelry. The 53-mile (85-kilometer) Vasa Cross-country Ski Marathon (*Vasaloppet*) takes place on the first Sunday in March, in Mora. It re-creates the flight of Gustav Vasa in 1520 after the "Stockholm Blood Bath."

If the great outdoors does not appeal, there are

film festivals in Stockholm in November and Gothenburg in late January/early February.

NATIONAL DAY

Sweden's National Day on June 6, originally called Flag Day, actually marks the accession of Gustav I Vasa as King of Sweden in 1523. It is characterized by the public display of flags and a ceremony at Skansen, the open-air museum-park in Stockholm, where the King presents flags to representatives of various civic groups. It is a regular, working day.

AWARD CEREMONIES

Polar Music Prize: May

The late Stig Anderson, Abba's manager and lyricist, created the Polar Music Prize to honor exceptional

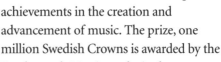 achievements in the creation and advancement of music. The prize, one million Swedish Crowns is awarded by the

King of Sweden each May in a televised ceremony.

Stockholm Water Prize: August

The US $150,000 Stockholm Water Prize is awarded each August during the annual World Water Week by its patron, the King of Sweden, to the person or organization that has done the most for the betterment of the world's water quality.

Nobel Day: December 10

Funded in 1896 by an endowment from Alfred Nobel, the Nobel Prizes acknowledge excellence in literature, physics, chemistry, medicine, and physiology at a special ceremony in Stockholm each year on December 10, the anniversary of Nobel's death. The Nobel Peace Price is awarded simultaneously in Oslo, reflecting the former union of Sweden and Norway in Nobel's lifetime. The occasion is televised internationally.

FAMILY OCCASIONS

Birth, Baptism, and Confirmation

Until recently, if one parent was a Lutheran a child born in Sweden automatically became a member of the Church of Sweden. Today, 75 percent of children in Sweden are baptized in the Church of Sweden, usually after the regular Sunday services. Only 55 percent of all fifteen-year-olds elect to be confirmed. They may go to confirmation camp, or they may be confirmed in their own  church. Following christening and confirmation ceremonies, friends and relatives attend a reception in the home, bringing presents.

Graduation

Graduation from *gymnasium*, the Swedish equivalent of the American high school, is a big occasion. On graduation day family and friends gather outside the school in groups with a large placard or poster on a tall stick, bearing an enlarged photo of the graduate at a young age. When the graduates emerge, miniature "splits" of sparkling wine tied with blue and yellow ribbons are draped around their necks. Soon, a caravan of decorated antique cars, flatbed trucks, and convertibles, complete with live bands and loud sound systems, winds through the streets. The graduates eventually arrive at the staid family reception their parents are giving in their honor, and later move on for a party of their own.

Engagement

Engaged couples exchange gold bands, worn on the left hand. The woman will receive a second gold band at the wedding ceremony.

Traditionally, on the Sunday before the wedding there was an afternoon dinner in the bride's home (*lysning*). Guests would bring their wedding presents to this occasion, rather than to the wedding itself.

Some time before the wedding day, girlfriends of the bride-to-be "kidnap" her for a day, all in great fun, and put her through various amusing situations in public. This "hen's" surprise party (*möhippa*) concludes with a dinner and much drinking and socializing as the girls wish her well. The male equivalent is the "stag" party (*svensexa*).

Weddings

Most weddings take place in church. The couple walk up the aisle together before the ceremony, rather than the bride's father escorting her to the waiting groom. After the wedding, the newlyweds stand outside in the churchyard in a receiving line. A dinner follows, usually in another location, and the newlyweds, who were the last to arrive, stay quite late to enjoy the fun.

Civil marriages became legal in 1908 and constitute one-third of all weddings today. Homosexual marriages, recognized in 1995, are performed as civil ceremonies.

During the wedding dinner there is much toasting and ribbing of the newlyweds, with old friends relating amusing or embarrassing stories. The first dance is danced by the newlyweds. Guests dance with their dinner partners first, and then, much later, with their spouses or accompanying partner. Women guests do not wear black to weddings. It is considered bad luck.

Birthdays

Being pragmatic people, the Swedes assume responsibility for their own birthday celebrations. At work, a person brings in his own cake and invites colleagues to join him.

Birthdays ending in a "0"—and especially 50 and onward—are particularly important and often celebrated in great style, with much good-natured speech-making and toasting. The celebrant might alternatively dispense with the party and go away on a special trip.

Some Swedes also celebrate their "name days." Each day of the year has a particular name or names associated with it.

Funerals

Death notices are published in the newspaper, listing the time and location of the church service. Those planning to attend the reception following the service are asked to call the company handling the funeral arrangements. Many people today are cremated—a more practical solution, since months can go by before the ground has thawed enough for the deceased person to be buried.

Mourners file past the closed coffin. Each pauses to lay a single flower on top of it, looks solemnly and reflectively down, and then continues around and back to his pew.

RELIGION

Although 82 percent of the population belong to the Evangelical Lutheran Church, only 5 percent attend church regularly. In many respects, the Church has gone the way of the monarchy, serving primarily a ceremonial role. Many of the old traditions it sanctioned are dying out, baptism, confirmation, and marriage being just a few examples. Other religious groups, all very small, include Roman Catholics, Pentecostals, Muslims, and Jews. Institutionalized religion, in the minds of many, has been replaced by communion with nature—boating, hiking, mushroom picking, and simply sitting and looking out over a beautiful scene.

chapter four

MAKING FRIENDS

All Swedes today learn English at school from a young age. On one level, this means that it is very easy for the visitor to communicate, but this is deceptive. Although Swedes are charming and helpful to strangers, on a longer-term basis they are reticent, and slow to make new friends. Until the advent of inexpensive flights, travel outside the country was less common, so ideas, attitudes, and social habits were quite insular.

For a visitor to move beyond acquaintanceship to friendship requires patience. The Swedes are considerably less loquacious than people from countries further south. Those who are widely traveled are more open and spontaneous.

Swedish conversation has an exchange pattern all its own, and foreigners, especially those from North America, tend to go wrong by offering too much information too soon. The conversational comfort zone of a Swede follows a certain cadence: a brief question followed by a brief answer. The length and strength of the response should match the question.

WORK AND SOCIAL LIFE

The Swedes do not mix business and pleasure on a personal basis by going out for a drink after work with colleagues. They tend to have a few close friends whom they have known from university or from childhood. Once a Swede forms a friendship, however, it usually endures. These things are taken seriously.

Team-building is an important concept, however, and Swedish companies often host elaborate corporate parties, outings, or weekend getaways (employees, no spouses) as a way of bringing people together on a personal level—at the company's expense! An overnight ski trip, golf outing, all-night birthday party (one of the "0's" such as forty or fifty), or an overnight boat cruise aboard a ferry to Finland, are all ways of breaking down the barriers in the Swedish workplace.

Professional networking events, popular in the U.S.A. as a way of meeting potential social partners, come across rather stiffly in Sweden. It is very un-Swedish to walk up to a relative stranger and initiate a conversation.

If the workplace is not a source of social contacts, how then does one meet Swedes? They are extremely health-conscious, and they love being outdoors. If they don't belong to a local gym or health club, they participate in community workout groups in a public park or school gymnasium, or they belong to a sports club, such as an outdoor ice-skating club in the winter, or a golf or tennis club. There are numerous walking and jogging paths, but the extremes in climate make it challenging to jog outdoors in the wintertime. Orienteering, a cross-country competition where the runners navigate through the woods using their compasses against a stopwatch, is a popular sport.

It is not uncommon for husbands and wives to have separate nights out—something the visitor should be aware of. Swedish women expect the same freedom as their partners, and take it.

The Swedes have enquiring minds, and many take courses, for example in languages, antiques, or handicrafts, or participate in choral groups. For long-term visitors, such activities as these provide good opportunities to meet people.

Dating Etiquette

Dating can be a confusing experience for visitors to Sweden. Because of the equality of the sexes, it is not uncommon for couples up to the age of fifty to split the bill equally, or even to arrive separately. They feel that this releases them from any preconceived notions of obligation as to how the evening might end.

CLOTHING

Clothing in Sweden is rarely dressy. For the average Swede in daily work life, casual clothing, such as jeans with sweaters or pullovers, is the norm. A managerial-level person might wear a sports jacket instead of a sweater with his jeans. Colors are dark (usually black) or neutral; fabrics are natural, such as cotton or wool. Sandals (with socks), tennis shoes, and hiking boots are favored by the younger set, boat shoes or boots by the older person. There is a sort of reverse snobbism when it comes to clothes: clothes do not make the person; intelligence does.

The Swedes are fond of saying, "There is no bad weather—only bad clothes." Warm clothing, gloves, and warm boots with thick waterproof soles are essential. A second pair of shoes is often brought and put on indoors. Hats are highly recommended in the winter.

While some professionals, such as lawyers, bankers, and CEOs (called VDs for *verkställande direktör*) wear suits and ties, the rest of Sweden dresses for comfort and functionality both on the job and off. Physicians may wear casual clothes and sandals or clogs, thick, wooden-soled shoes, with socks. Television announcers rarely have clothing budgets, so they, too, dress simply. The largest single employer in Sweden is the government, and in an egalitarian society no one should appear to be any wealthier than anyone else. This goes full-circle back to the Jante Laws described in Chapter 2.

If you are traveling to Sweden for an interview or business meeting, dress plainly and conservatively. Forgo denim. Basic black will see you through almost any situation.

Dressing Up

For the business traveler there are three types of invitation that merit attention.

Invitations for dinner parties usually specify *kavaj* (which means dark or dark blue suits for men). For women, it means a conservative but fashionable dinner suit or pantsuit with good jewelry.

Dressy events, which are rare, are specified as *smoking* (tuxedo/black tie) for a man. *Högtidsdräkt* or nothing written on the invitation means *tails* (white tie) for the man, and a long dress for the woman. Subdued classics are preferred to high fashion in bright colors. Glittery, sequined dresses are rarely seen.

GREETINGS

Swedish is such an efficient language that one word suffices for both hello and good-bye: *Hej!* (pronounced "hay!"). Good-bye may be a more

effusive version: *hej då* (pronounced "hay door").
The expressions "please" and "thank you" are
equally efficient: *Tack* says it all.

Swedes rarely address a person as Mr. or Mrs.
unless they are quite elderly. First names are used.
They are also not big on titles, such as "President"
or "Managing Director," since in the model
society no one is any better than anyone else.
Business cards in Sweden often will only give the
person's name, unlike in America or Britain.

In both business and social settings, it is
customary to shake hands and simultaneously
say your own name. In social
settings, the most recent person
arriving makes the rounds of
those already present and
introduces himself. Eye
contact is important.

VISITORS ARE WELCOME
Almost all shopkeepers under the age of about
sixty speak English. That does not necessarily
imply a nuanced command of the language but,
rather, a functional use. Most Swedes enjoy the
opportunity to practice their English on visitors.
However, if you have not grown up in a bilingual
culture, it is worth remembering that speaking a
second language on a prolonged basis can be

taxing to someone with average proficiency.

Visitors to Sweden are more easily accepted than immigrants, since they will soon be leaving and will not burden the social service system. Up to a point, there is no expectation that the visitor should attempt to learn a language spoken by only nine million people; however, if the visit turns into residency, most Swedes feel the newcomer should learn Swedish and become an integrated part of Swedish society. Free, government-funded language and lifestyle courses are offered to both temporary and permanent residents.

One of the oddities of life in Sweden is that native English speakers find themselves treated with much more courtesy and respect in retail situations if they speak English, even if they are studying Swedish. As a result the Swedish-language student becomes more motivated to continue to speak English than to torture himself and his listeners with his halting Swedish.

JOINING CLUBS

The Swedes are great joiners. If you would like to meet them in their element, consider joining an activity group or club. Choirs (church or secular) and sports groups, such as exercise groups that meet in a local park, and long-distance ice skating groups, are very popular.

Golf courses in Sweden require Swedes to have a special "green card," signifying knowledge of the rules and an entry-level competency. Public and private courses, however, will accept foreign guest players as long as they are convinced that the player has a modicum of proficiency and, for insurance reasons, membership in a club. Often, the handicap level will be 33 or 35. There are also "pay and play" courses that have no restrictions.

English-speakers can also join expatriate groups such as the British Commonwealth Club; the American Club of Sweden, which recently merged with American Citizens Abroad in Sweden; the American Women's Club; the English-Speaking Community Club; the International Women's Club; various Chambers of Commerce, such as AmCham (the Swedish American Chamber of Commerce), the British-Swedish Chamber of Commerce, and the Canadian Swedish Business Association; and under certain conditions, various diplomatic clubs. Most of these clubs are based in the capital city of Stockholm. There are also American Women's Clubs in Gothenburg, Malmö, and Kristianstad. The easiest way to locate these clubs is via the appropriate embassy or on the Internet.

INVITATIONS HOME

In-home entertaining is much more common than going out to restaurants. To be invited into a Swedish home is a real honor. Guests usually bring a gift of flowers, candy, or wine. When giving flowers, the Swedes like to pretend that they are straight from the garden, and will remove and hide the florist's paper before knocking on your door. Wines and spirits can only be purchased at state-owned stores that are part of the "System"—*Systemet*, short for *Systembolaget*. Until recently you could not buy alcohol on Saturdays, or after 6:00 p.m. on weekdays.

As we have seen, punctuality is extremely important, but don't arrive early. Be on time. If you are unavoidably detained, you should call ahead and alert the host. "Late" in Sweden is anything not exactly on time. You will be offered one "welcome drink" upon arrival, and the dinner will be served exactly on time. Latecomers will spoil the meal.

You will rarely be seated with your escort or companion. The Swedes feel it is much more stimulating to get people talking as individuals, rather than as couples, who tend to form one conversational unit when seated together. The guest of honor is seated to the left of the hostess. If there is no hostess, then the main guest sits to the left of the host. The man to the left of any female guest is her *kavaljer*, from the French *cavalier*, whose duty it is to attend to her needs. This escort service continues throughout the entire evening, not just at the dinner table.

Prior to leaving the table, the guest of honor is expected to give a few witty remarks thanking the hostess for dinner.

The Toasting Ritual

No one drinks before the host has proposed a toast. Following the host's example, everyone takes exactly one mouthful of the starter and expectantly puts their knives and forks at rest on their plates. The host raises his glass of wine and offers a welcoming toast, saying how glad he is that you could all be present tonight.

The toasting ritual is rather prescribed: hold your glass near your breastbone at about the level of the third button on a shirt. Once your host has finished his welcome remarks and said "*Skål!*" (pronounced "skoal"), raise your glass and tip it slightly toward him while saying the same thing. Slowly make eye contact with every single person around the table, one after the other. Then, in synchronization with your host, take one sip of the wine, return the glass to the chest-high position, and again make eye contact with him, and then with each guest around the table before putting your glass down. You are now free to drink at will, and do not need to wait for further toasts. A man can genteelly flirt with a woman (or several women at different times) during the evening by duplicating this toasting ritual on a one-to-one basis, which can be quite fun. Note: Swedes never clink glasses!

Remember that Swedes, like other Europeans, eat with the fork in the left hand and the knife in the right. The American custom of "cutting and switching" utensils is considered childish! Salad follows the meal. Then comes the cheese and fruit course, often with several types of cheese offered.

One of the less elegant aspects of dining in Sweden is the communal butter knife. One takes a piece of butter on the knife and spreads it on one's bread before returning it to the butter dish. Do not be surprised if a knifeful of butter is passed to you. This is not so common at formal dinner parties, but it is otherwise quite normal. Also note that the Swedes rarely touch their food with their fingers—even in eating something as ordinary as pizza or a cheeseburger!

Throughout the dinner, while much wine will be offered, not everyone will partake. The reason is Sweden's extremely strict drunk-driving laws (see page 120). One weak drink is the maximum before one is legally "under the influence," and the penalties are severe. Thus, either one member of a couple is the designated driver, or the couple takes a taxi, in which case both can drink.

After the meal the guests may be invited to retire to the living room for dessert, coffee, and after-dinner drinks. This is a more comfortable way of prolonging the evening, and constitutes a major part of the evening's entertainment.

Other than dinner parties, another form of home entertaining is the afternoon coffee party, or *fika*, characterized by several types of dessert, good, strong coffee, and friendly conversation. Coffee is the fuel that keeps Sweden running— in the office, at home, everywhere. The Swedes are among the largest consumers of coffee in the world. The Christmas-time variation on the *fika* is the mulled wine party, or *glögg* party, with ginger cookies and holiday treats.

GIFT GIVING

Office colleagues rarely give birthday or anniversary gifts; they will, on a rare occasion, take up a collection of a few kronor (the equivalent of, say, a couple of dollars) and buy a wedding gift. Even though the standard of living is quite high, most people do not have a lot of discretionary money due to high taxation.

The same holds true in the exchange of birthday and Christmas gifts between friends. The sentiment is more important than the cost, and often a token gift, especially something of a practical nature, is more comfortably received than something expensive or frivolous. The exception might be a present for someone celebrating one of the "0" birthdays, where the festivities are often quite elaborate and can be expensive. Birthday parties are given by the celebrants, not their friends.

Hostess gifts such as flowers, wine, or candy, as we have seen, are customary. Alcohol is generally expensive and therefore is appreciated. Travelers from outside the Eurozone can buy it less expensively through duty-free shops.

EMILY POST COMES TO SWEDEN

The Swedes are some of the most congenial hosts in the world; they take care to make their guests feel welcome and part of the group. Age is a great factor in the Swedish woman's receptivity to gentlemanly courtesies, such as opening doors, holding out chairs, standing when the lady rises, and so forth. The more mature Swedish man will chivalrously do all of these things for a woman, but on occasion these gallantries are misunderstood or underappreciated by Swedish women. The younger generation has dispensed with a lot of these customs because Swedish women have been taught to be self-sufficient and to consider themselves equal to men. Men, therefore, tread lightly, not knowing if their courtesies will be well received or not.

Thank-you notes or phone calls to a hostess are always appreciated. The customary greeting when talking to someone who has hosted you earlier is to say, "Thanks for the last time." Regardless of nationality, one would like to think that good manners are eternal.

chapter five

THE SWEDES AT HOME

QUALITY OF LIFE

The Swedes love their homes, and this is apparent the moment you enter them. Candles softly glow, lighting is subdued, and fresh flowers lend an air of cheeriness. The whole effect is cozy, welcoming, restful, and harmonious, for the Swedes, when not outdoors, happily spend a lot of time at home.

The Swedes have conquered winter, at least indoors. Their houses and apartments are well-insulated and well-heated, and windows are double-glazed and caulked against drafts.

One unusual aspect of winter is the danger of the sudden falling of long, pointed icicles and heavy masses of snow from the rooftops. Building owners are required to remove these and to warn pedestrians of the potential danger by placing special signs or barricades on the sidewalks. Snow removal from the streets is excellent, and in some parts of Stockholm the sidewalks are heated.

The Swedes are extremely conscientious about recycling. Each neighborhood has an area with bins for newsprint, cardboard, tin cans, colored

and clear glass, hard plastic, and batteries.
Households have separate containers for each.
Packaging materials, and even gift wrap, will often
be biodegradable.

LIVING CONDITIONS

Of the 8.9 million people living in Sweden, nearly
a third live in and around the cities of Stockholm,
Gothenburg, and Malmö. Slightly more than 50
percent of the population live in houses; the rest
live in apartments. There are also approximately
580,000 vacation houses.

Apartments in city centers can be very small by
American standards. Stockholm's Gamla Stan
(Old Town) dates back to the thirteenth century
and contains 2,014 dwelling units, of which 2,007
are apartments. Thirty-one percent of these are
one-room "studio" apartments.

In some of these conversions bathrooms have
been created from former closets, and do not
always have bathtubs. Visitors are often amazed to
discover "the Swedish shower"—a completely
tiled bathroom with a sealed, waterproof floor
sloping to a drainage hole.

Modern apartments are larger and better
appointed. Small apartments are compensated for
by large communal areas including party rooms,
storage space, and laundry facilities. (Public

laundromats with coin-operated washers and driers are unknown.) Some buildings have communal saunas and tanning beds. Residents are expected to keep common areas free of clutter, although there is great tolerance of the baby carriage—children are sacred.

The notion of communal space also extends to the airwaves. If you are having a party, it is courteous to post a notice advising your neighbors—or, better, to invite them. If the party is too noisy, you may receive a visit from a local security company. These investigate disturbances and, if necessary, make limited arrests.

People live in close proximity in the city, and learn to give each other privacy by not being overly friendly or intrusive, or staring at their neighbors on the balcony.

Don't Look!

An American visitor commented to a Swedish friend that her neighbor walked around naked without drawing the curtains. Her Swedish friend responded that the onus was on her not to look!

While space may be at a premium and salaries modest, the Swedes enjoy their creature comforts, prioritizing these expenditures, whether by cash or by credit, over other types of purchases. These include state-of-the-art electronics, such as televisions, digital disc players, computers, telephones, and stereo components.

LANDSCAPE AND ARCHITECTURE

Most apartment buildings in Stockholm are built directly on the sidewalk, with each building's side walls touching the next. Older apartment complexes often form a quadrangle around a grassy interior courtyard. In good weather, these hidden areas provide a delightful green oasis for residents to relax in with a good book and a cup of coffee or a glass of wine. They also offer enthusiasts the opportunity to do a little inner-city gardening.

Because so much of Sweden is surrounded by water, homes are oriented to capture as much of the view as possible. Light, also, is precious, and large expanses of window are common. Throughout Sweden, there is always a vista awaiting, whether it is a beautiful mountain range, an unspoiled, rolling field, or a waterfront stretching out to infinity.

RENTING VS. BUYING

Most Swedes own their apartment or house and there is very little property available to rent, particularly in Stockholm. Since rent control was initiated at the end of the Second World War, rental apartment housing has not been a part of the market economy, and supply, therefore, has not kept up with demand.

Government-subsidized rental apartments have long waiting lists. Private owners may rent out or lease their apartments, but they must comply with the rates set by the rent control authorities. They also must have the permission of their condominium association. Many will only permit a condo owner to rent his apartment for a maximum of one year, after which he must resume living in the apartment himself, or sell it.

The black market is the midpoint between renting and buying. It is possible to buy a black-market lease in Sweden, but illegal to sell one because of rent control. Since the official rental rate of the lease you might buy is lower than the market rent, you must pay cash "under the table" to make up the difference. You are not in violation of the law in doing this; the seller is.

Rented properties come furnished or unfurnished, with short-term rentals more commonly furnished. A time-specific lease is the norm. Because of the paucity of rental properties, a lease may often specify a three-month written notice of nonrenewal by either party.

One problem North Americans may encounter

is that landlords and banks may be unable to do credit checks on their overseas financial history. If this happens, have a reputable friend or your employer vouch for you. Try to avoid looking for property during December and January. Most Swedes will be totally preoccupied with holiday entertaining. For anyone coming to Sweden for an extended stay, long-term rental properties are hard to find; short-term (three-month) are more numerous because they are "second-hand," that is, a tenant subletting his own furnished apartment. Most newspaper ads will be for trades between people who already have apartments and want to move (larger, smaller, new neighborhood or city). While properties for sale generally are shown via an open house, properties to rent do not usually have public viewing, and disappear from the market almost immediately. If you find something even remotely suitable, grab it.

One recommendation is to develop a list of real estate offices and call them mercilessly *before* the ads are published each week. However, even knowing that you are a ready, willing, and able tenant, they usually will not return your calls. Alternately, hire an agency that specializes in finding rental properties.

Furnishings and Appliances

Stoves and refrigerators are usually provided with the apartment; lighting fixtures often are not. Most rentals include a monthly fee paid to the apartment association for heat and hot water. The heat is centrally controlled by the condo association, but you will be able to regulate it within your own apartment. Gas and electric costs are payable by the tenant to the utility companies, as are cable television and broadband Internet connections. Telephone installation is an easy matter and accomplished within a couple of days with the flick of a switch in the central office. Many short-term rentals will come complete with a working telephone line, as the owners do not want to lose their number while away.

Swedish electrical current is 220 volts, and it requires a two-pronged, round plug. The sockets are recessed. Even if you adapt the plug, American electrical appliances will not work without a converter (from U.S. 110 volt to European 220). British people merely need to change their three-pronged plugs to the two-pronged round style.

Many computers now come with built-in current converters, but it is always wise to check before risking a meltdown. To connect to the Internet via a Swedish telephone jack, you will need a special adapter.

IDENTITY CARDS AND RESIDENCY

All Swedes are issued with an identity card showing their photo and personal number. The *personnummer* functions like a social security number in America or Britain. The cards are used to verify your identity when making purchases via credit card, seeing a doctor or dentist (because of the government health subsidy as well as for safety reasons), registering for school, or for banking (including opening a bank account). Visitors may stay up to three months in Sweden as a tourist and use their passports as identity cards. This may be extended by another three months on application to the immigration authorities, but in no circumstances are you allowed to stay more than six months without either a temporary or permanent residency permit.

Temporary residency may be granted for up to one year at a time, and is often used by those with corporate transfers. It must be renewed each year via the immigration office. Permanent residency for non-EU citizens is difficult to obtain, and is usually granted for one of two reasons: a relationship, such as marriage or parenthood, and political sanctuary. Often the permit for non-EU citizens is only for six months at a time, unless it is related to a firm contract of employment. Application for residency should be made prior to leaving your home country. If you wish to work in

Sweden, a work visa is necessary and is usually obtained at the same time. EU citizens have a right to a Swedish work permit, and may be granted a three-month residency in which to secure work. As with any government paperwork, all this can take time. You will need proof of residency in order to apply for a "person number."

FAMILY LIFE AND ROUTINES

The Swedes get up early, around 6:30–7:00 a.m., and, if working in an office, are usually there by 8:00 or 8:30 a.m. Breakfast could be oatmeal porridge, bread or crispbread and butter, with ham, salami, cheese, and perhaps cucumber or tomato. There could be hard- or soft-boiled eggs, yogurt, fruit, orange juice, milk, tea, or coffee.

Day-care centers for children aged one to six are open from 6:30 a.m. to 6:30 p.m. There are also part-time groups for children aged four to six and preschools. Compulsory "basic" schools (ages seven to sixteen) run Monday through Friday, eight hours a day for older students and six for younger, with the exact calendar and times established by the respective municipalities. Students eat lunch at school. Children aged six to twelve often participate in extracurricular programs at after-school centers.

Many Swedes eat a substantial hot meal at

lunchtime. Restaurants commonly offer inexpensive daily specials that typically include bread and butter, a salad, a main course, and a beverage, usually light beer, a fruit-flavored cold drink made from syrup (called *saft*), coffee, or tea.

The Swedish coffee culture brings together mothers and young children for an afternoon coffee party (*fika*) of conversation, pastries, and desserts. Be prepared for robust flavor: the Swedes call American coffee "brown water."

Supper can be an early affair, around 6:00 or 6:30 p.m. for those who have gone to work by 8:00 a.m., 7:30 or 8:00 p.m. for those who work later hours, or if there are guests for dinner. Bedtime is around 10:30 or 11:00 p.m. on weeknights.

BOUNDS AND BOUNDARIES

Modern Swedish homes tend to have open floor plans in the common areas, such as the living room and dining room, and the kitchen is always a welcome place where people lend a helping hand. Heating in all Swedish homes is excellent, and there is no need to shut doors to conserve it. The bedrooms, however, are private. Rarely would a guest be given a formal tour of the house. Generally speaking, guests should stay in the room where they were brought, and let their host set the boundaries. Good manners do not change

that much from country to country, and
sensitivity to personal space is always appreciated.

Shoe Etiquette

In many Swedish homes it is customary to remove
your shoes at the door to avoid tracking in water,
mud, or gravel. Many people bring a pair of light
shoes to change into. Plan ahead! It may be
embarrassing to find a hole in your sock because
you forgot you would be taking off your shoes!

SHARING THE BURDEN

Swedish women and men share parenting and
household management fairly equally. Men often
cook, take care of the children, do the laundry,
and iron their own shirts. Society expects a
woman to be able to support herself, to have some
security against becoming a widow or divorcee or
otherwise being dependent on the support of the
state. Few women are simply housewives, even if
they are well off, as the norm is for women to be
actively engaged in something meaningful.

During the early childhood years, it usually is
the woman who stays at home with the babies. As
the stay-at-home parent, she gets 80 percent of
her salary (with a ceiling) for the first 390 days of

the baby's life, and a nominal sum for the next ninety days. Sixty days are reserved (mandatory leave) for the baby's father. The mother is guaranteed her job back once she returns to work.

The foreign woman marrying a Swedish man will be pleasantly surprised that he is so enlightened; the foreign man, by contrast, may be somewhat taken aback by his self-sufficient Swedish wife, who will expect complete equality. In the family hierarchy the child is sacred, and both parents will put the child's needs ahead of their own. Most Swedes adore children and treat them like little adults. This can be challenging when they are brought to dinner parties!

SCHOOLS AND SCHOOLING

Subsidized day care *(dagis)* and preschool *(förskola)* are provided for young children. From the age of six, all Swedish children attend school *(grundskolan)* for nine years. After this, a student chooses a specialized program of studies for his final three years at what Americans call "high school" *(gymnasium)*. Swedish schools emphasize teamwork over individual achievement.

Those *gymnasium* graduates with good grades

may elect to attend a technical college (*högskola*), such as the Royal Technical School (*Kungliga Tekniska Högskolan*, or KTH) or the Stockholm School of Economics (*Handelshögskolan*, known as HHS); or a state university, such as Uppsala or Lund. A Swedish bachelor's degree takes three years, and a master's degree takes four to four-and-a-half years to complete. Tuition is free; room and board are not. Most students take low-interest loans and live away from home.

The government also subsidizes a series of courses to retrain unemployed people in skills needed for the marketplace. It also provides free Swedish-language courses for immigrants via its Swedish for Immigrants (*Svenska för Invandrare*, or SFI) program, and "mother tongue" language courses for *gymnasium* students whose parents speak another language at home. Swedish adults who never finished school may attend a people's school (*folkhögskola*), as a boarder or day student, to obtain a *gymnasium* equivalency certificate.

Nonconfrontation

While the Swedes may, like anyone else, be critical, dissatisfied, or disapproving of certain things, they will rarely be confrontational in their way of dealing with them. They do not show any extremes of emotion. They are honest and direct, but not aggressive in style. They use exclusion to express disapproval of behavior. As a group action, this type of peer pressure is effective.

Parents are forbidden by law to strike a child. Yet every parent at some point encounters the whining or angry, crying child who will not be quiet. The Swedish solution is to ignore the bad behavior, speak calmly and rationally, and continue onward. Rarely will you see a parent yell at the child in anger.

CHANGING LIFESTYLES

Punctual, orderly, and calm, the Swedes are happiest when everything runs smoothly and on time, without any rough edges. Their homes are relaxing and welcoming—tastefully appointed little islands of tranquillity that buffer them from the cold, dark world outside. Perhaps some of the external trappings of the old lifestyles are changing—certainly, young couples cohabit rather than marry, commune with nature rather than the Church, and conceive children who may be raised in day-care centers rather than at home. But throughout it all, the fundamental values remain. Sweden is still one of the most progressive, egalitarian, and unspoiled countries in the world. Some call it a well-kept secret. Many would like to keep it that way.

chapter six

TIME OUT

The Swedes enjoy more free time than most Americans dream of. With five weeks' paid vacation, twelve paid holidays, numerous "squeeze days" when a holiday falls midweek, and various slow-down periods around the summer and winter solstices, Sweden really is a worker's paradise. Add to this, for those in the childrearing/bearing years, up to 480 days paid parental leave upon the birth of a child, generous paid sick leave, and a workweek that rarely entails overtime, and you have a pretty idyllic situation by anyone's standards, except the employers'.

SHOPPING

Overall, the Swedes are functional rather than recreational shoppers. The exception to this is food shopping at food halls such as Östermalmshallen, in the upscale section of Stockholm, where you can buy the most fresh, most select meats, cheeses, fish, poultry, fruit, and vegetables, and baked goods at heartstopping prices. Within this food hall, as within others in the Hötorget and Södermalm sections of the city, there are also a few restaurants and coffee bars. All Swedes believe that fresh food is preferable to frozen. In the nearby outdoor marketplaces, you can find fresh flowers and other seasonal items.

In very small shops the proprietor might greet you, but, by and large, the Swedes leave you to yourself. Shopkeepers and sales people are not commission-driven, so most of the time it is irrelevant to them whether you make a purchase or not. Therefore, lower your expectations of service if you want to be a happier shopper.

SOME USEFUL SHOPS

Konditori Bakery cum coffee shop

Apoteket Pharmacy (sells both prescription medicines and over-the-counter health aids)

Matäffar Supermarket. Well-known chains are ICA, Vivo, and Konsum. Swedish supermarkets are rarely as large as their U.S. equivalents.

Saluhall Food hall. Marketplace with various specialty shops, such as butcher, bakery, coffee and tea boutique, fresh fish shop and so on, all under one roof.

Kemtvätt Dry cleaners

Shopping Hours

Most shops are open from 10:00 a.m. to 6:00 p.m., Monday through Friday, with shops in the larger city centers often open until 7:00 p.m. On Saturdays most shops are open until 2:00 p.m., with larger department stores in the three main cities open until 5:00 p.m. Sunday hours vary: large department stores, shopping malls, and some shops in larger city centers are open on Sunday, usually from 12:00 to 4:00 p.m., but the hours are not standardized. The huge shopping malls that are so prevalent in American suburbs are rare in Sweden. Larger supermarkets are open until 8:00 or 9:00 p.m. even on Sundays; the colorful food halls are not open on Sundays, and have limited hours on Saturdays. There are quite a few legal holidays, and many stores close on these days—especially if the holiday has religious overtones.

BANKS AND CURRENCY EXCHANGE

Banks in Sweden are open normally from 9:30 a.m. to 3:00 p.m., and some banks will stay open once a week until 6:00 p.m. All banks are closed on Saturdays, Sundays, and legal holidays—and on the day before a holiday! Note: during the very last days of December, most banks will close down altogether so as to give a good, clean finish to the current financial year.

ATM or automated cash machines are plentiful through the cities. Swedes use a bank debit card with a PIN code. Visitors (non-Swedes) may withdraw money from these cash machines using a conventional Visa/MasterCard, for which there is a nominal service charge.

Sweden rejected joining the European Monetary Union in September 2003, and is not expected to revive the issue of joining until 2010. Therefore, the unit of currency is still the Swedish krona. If you are exchanging money, your best bet cost-wise is a *bureau de change* rather than a bank or hotel. You can also change money at the airport, the Central Station (train), and the tourist office. Be sure to take a number from the *nummerlapp* dispensing machine.

All stores and taxi cabs take the common credit cards, such as Visa and MasterCard; many also take American Express. Travelers' checks are accepted in some, but not all, stores. Note: the state monopoly liquor stores accept only Swedish credit cards or cash.

More and more Swedish people use debit cards rather than cash within their own country because they are so easy, convenient, and universally accepted. The use of printed checks by Swedes is a thing of the past.

Shopping Tips for Tourists

Sales tax—VAT, called *moms* in Sweden—is 25 percent, with the exception of food, which is

12 percent, and medicine, which is not taxed. Tourists from non-EU countries are entitled to receive 15–18 percent of the sales tax back when they leave the country, provided that the cost of each item purchased exceeds SEK 200. The store must be a member of Global Refund Sverige. Ask for a special Global Refund Check before you pay for your purchase. You exchange this check for cash at a duty-free window at the airport when you leave Sweden, or at your last point of departure from the EU. Your goods must be exported within three months of purchase, and the adhesive seal on the package must be intact.

Clean lines and natural materials distinguish contemporary Swedish designs in wood, glass, and metal. The cutting edge of modern Swedish design is the store Svenskt Tenn in Stockholm.

Sweden is world-famous for its crystal. For an unforgettable combination of price and selection, often at one-third the cost in Swedish big city stores, take a trip to the Kingdom of Crystal, Sweden's glass country, located in Småland in the south.

The classically painted red Dalecarlia wooden horse, and hand-painted wooden clogs are both popular and typical examples of folk art, as are Sami handicrafts (marked *Duodji* to signify authenticity). Hand knits and woven textiles, especially linen, are simple and beautiful.

Swedish food specialties include wild berry preserves, especially lingonberries, for meatballs, and cloudberries (*hjortron*), which are wonderful when warm and served over ice cream.

Typical drinks are *Absolut* vodka, flavored *snaps* gift-packed as miniatures, and mulled wine (*glögg*) at Christmas.

Christmas markets abound in the four weeks of Advent that lead up to Christmas. See www.stockholmtown.com/events for listings of Christmas markets as well as other happenings in the capital city and neighboring archipelago.

Twice a year, from just after Christmas until the end of January, and from late June through the end of July, there are big sales in the major cities. The magic word in Swedish is *rea* (sale!).

Finally, there is a thriving antiques market in both Stockholm and Gothenburg, the oldest and most prominent auction house being Bukowskis. Stockholm also is home to the company Auktionsverket, which handles both quality and more affordable items. Some auction items considered particular to Swedish culture are excluded from export, but these are clearly marked.

Waiting in Line

Regulated by moderation and orderliness in all things, the Swedes have an accepted way of lining

up to make purchases that relies on each buyer
taking a number from the *nummerlapp* machine.

Open Purchase *(Öppet Köp)*

It is difficult to return purchased goods in Sweden
unless you specifically request what is known as
an "open purchase" (*öppet köp*), or unless the
store automatically has this as a policy. If there is
some question in your mind that you might need
to return the item, ask first. Note: do not just ask
if you can return an item. Be specific: you want to
return it and get a refund. The open purchase
policy allows you to return the merchandise
within a certain period, usually one week, for a
full cash refund; however, usually *öppet köp* must
be written or printed on the receipt. After that,
some shops will issue credit, but the policy is not
uniform throughout Sweden. Otherwise, unless
the item is damaged or defective, it is yours.

Alcohol Purchase

The only place in Sweden where one may buy
alcoholic beverages for take-out is at the
State-monopoly liquor stores, called "The
System Company," or simply "The System"
(*Systembolaget* or *Systemet*). (See
www.systembolaget.se.) *Systemet* store
hours are 9:30 or 10:00 a.m. until 6:00 or
7:00 p.m. weekdays, and there are limited

Saturday hours (10 a.m. to 2:00 or 3:00 p.m.) in some stores. The minimum age to purchase alcohol in the *Systemet* stores is twenty. Those traveling to non-EU countries may also purchase alcohol at the airport duty-free shop. "Hard" liquor, such as vodka, whiskey, and gin, is taxed according to its strength, making these beverages prohibitively expensive to purchase. Nearly 90 percent of the cost of a bottle of a type of schnapps called *brännvin*, for example, is tax.

RESTAURANTS, FOOD, AND DRINK

Because of its affinity with the sea, Sweden enjoys an abundance of fresh seafood throughout the year. One tasty native specialty is salmon (*lax*) served steamed, broiled, or pan-fried and topped with a herb sauce; cured in salt and dill as *gravad lax* (also spelled *gravlax*); or smoked and served cold with mustard sauce. You can also sample many types of caviar, and fresh little shrimp. Herring, pickled, marinated, or pan-fried is another favorite. Boiled potatoes, preferably the little new ones no larger than an egg, are very popular. In the winter season, wild game and reindeer are a special treat. Pork and chicken are staples at any time of year, and Swedish meatballs with mashed potatoes, gravy, and a "side" of tart lingonberry sauce are wonderful. Breads are hearty, natural-fiber loaves and hard crispbread. Ginger snap cookies (*pepparkakor*) at Christmas, whipped-cream-filled buns (*semla*) at Easter time, and fresh strawberries at the height of summer all leave indelible memories on the palate.

Because the Swedes value high-quality food made from fresh ingredients, "take-out" kitchens and fast-food restaurants are not common.

It is expensive to eat out at restaurants, and even more expensive to drink alcohol. When Swedes do eat out, they often will spend an entire evening at the restaurant. They think of it as entertainment. As a consequence, it can be difficult to secure a table in a popular restaurant by walking in off the street. If you are with a group of Swedes who are splitting the bill, remember that the Swedes value fairness. It is more common for each person to tally up his share than it is to divide the total amount equally. Restaurants are required to have nonsmoking areas. Because the Swedes are so health-conscious, however, fewer and fewer of them smoke.

A word to the wise: "Doggie-bag" devotees, beware! The Swedes frown upon the idea of taking leftovers away from restaurants. Most restaurants will humor you, but it is considered rather *déclassé* to ask for a doggie bag.

Waiters, Service, and Tipping

Since the waiter's or waitress's tip is already
factored into your bill, there is no great incentive
for him or her to do more than is required. Most
are very friendly and will provide you with an
English menu or a translation into English from
the Swedish, but basically the diner is considered a
purchaser of food and beverage, not service.
Attitudinally, "service" tends to get mixed up with
"servitude," a no-no in the land of equality.

Diners can round up the bill or add a small
amount if they feel the service was excellent, up to
a maximum of 10 percent, and preferably in cash,
which is "invisible." However, approximately
12 percent of the bill is already allocated as a tip.
On the positive side, you will never be pushed to
eat up so that the waiter can "turn the table," and,
once outside Sweden, you may find that you miss
the opportunity to sip that very long cup of coffee
while deep in conversation at the end of the meal.

Smörgåsbord Etiquette

The Swedish word *smörgåsbord* actually means
"sandwich table," but today it has come to mean a
self-service buffet filled with a variety of hot and
cold dishes, plus desserts. Most non-Swedes are
unaware of *smörgåsbord* etiquette and tend to
overindulge.

The *smörgåsbord* should be approached in

stages, and always with a clean plate for each course. Start with the cold dishes (fish first!), and do not mix fish with other, non-fishy foods. Then tackle the hot dishes, followed by a cheese and fruit plate, and then a sampling of the desserts. "Clean plate" means not only a clean plate for each course, but also a clean plate when you finish each course. It is considered impolite to waste food. In a Swedish *smörgåsbord*, you can return as many times as you like. The true delight is in the small, pure samplings of each course.

Drinking

Four different strengths of beer are available, and beer remains the most popular alcoholic beverage. Sweden has the second-highest consumption of coffee per capita in the world. Many 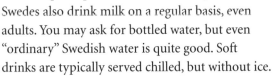 Swedes also drink milk on a regular basis, even adults. You may ask for bottled water, but even "ordinary" Swedish water is quite good. Soft drinks are typically served chilled, but without ice.

Wine consumption is on the rise. As members of Europe's "potato belt," the Swedes like vodka. Other popular alcoholic beverages are flavored *snaps*, *brännvin*, and *besk*; *punsch*, an arak-based sweet liqueur; and *glögg*, the Christmas-time favorite made from warm, spiced wine with a few raisins and blanched almonds added to each little mug prior to consumption. Note: Sweden has one of the toughest drunk-driving laws in the world. The maximum blood-alcohol limit of 0.02 percent equates to one glass of wine during an evening out, if you are driving.

As we have seen, the toasting ritual is usually initiated by the host after one mouthful of food at the beginning of a meal. The Swedish way of toasting is to say "*Skål!*" (pronounced "skoal"). Swedes do not clink glasses!

LEISURE

The Swedes love the great outdoors, even in the wintertime. The secret of surviving wintertime seasonal affective disorder (SAD), caused by months of bleak, dark weather, is to get outside at least once a day. They travel a lot, especially during the winter months, and group charter trips are both popular and inexpensive.

Sweden in the summertime, with its equally long periods of light, is fantastic, and no one needs urging to go outdoors. The Swedes also love gardening. Even city dwellers have small plots, called colony lots, allocated specifically for this.

Theme Parks and Tourist Attractions

There are a few Swedish theme parks, some dating to the late 1800s and 1920s. Stockholm's

Grönalund and Gothenburg's Liseberg are both modeled, in a fashion, on Copenhagen's famous Tivoli. They feature beer gardens, concert areas, restaurants, and rides, such as the roller coaster.

One hundred twenty-five miles (200 kilometers) north of the Arctic Circle in Lappland, tourists flock to the Ice Hotel, which is literally made of ice each winter and stays open until the ice melts, usually in April. The Swedish town of Mora, in Dalarna, nearer to the geographic center of Sweden, is the home of Santaworld (*Tomteland*), open from late November through New Year's Eve.

SPORTS

Physical fitness in Sweden is part of the national consciousness. There are some 22,000 officially registered sports clubs, as well as thousands of local clubs.

Popular Swedish sports include hunting, fishing, golf, tennis, ice-skating, skiing, bicycling, and water sports such as canoeing, kayaking, and sailing. The last weekend in May is Stockholm's *Tjejtrampet*, a 25-mile (40-kilometer) female-only bicycle race drawing 7,000 participants.

The *Vasaloppet* in Mora each March first started in 1922 with 119 competitors and now has some 15,000 participants and 50,000 spectators. Downhill skiing, while popular, especially in the areas of Åre and Sälen, is limited somewhat by the Swedish darkness and a lack of resorts.

Bandy, a sport unique to Sweden, is sometimes called winter's football. It is similar to ice hockey, with eleven players and a ball smaller than a tennis ball.

There are over 700 orienteering clubs, where cross-country runners, using a compass to fix navigation points, compete against a stopwatch.

Soccer (called "football" in Europe) has some 1,400 matches a day in Sweden. The country sports some 3,200 associations with over one million members.

Marathon runners also have their day: Gothenburg has the *Göteborgsvarvet*, a half-marathon in May, with over 35,000 runners. With some 13,000 participants, the Stockholm Marathon on the first Saturday in June is said to be one of the world's top ten. Unique to Sweden because of its long hours of daylight, Stockholm's Midnight Race in early August is a 6-mile (10 kilometer) race with 16,000 runners. In late August, the ladies are at it again in Stockholm with *Tjejmilen*, a 6-mile (10-kilometer) female-only road race with 25,000 runners.

For equestrians, the Stockholm International Horse Show, the biggest indoor horse show in the world, takes place in November.

HIGH CULTURE

Sweden is rich in museums. Stockholm alone has over fifty, including the royal museums in the Royal Palace, the Treasury, the Royal Armory, and the castles at Rosendal, Ulriksdal, Drottningholm, and the Pavillion of Gustav III in Haga Park. Other capital city museums highlight history, architecture, the Middle Ages, the Mediterranean and the Near East, Jewish history, the Far East, and ethnography. In southern Sweden, Kalmar Castle, dating back to the twelfth century, and the medieval walled city of Visby on the island of Gotland are both worth seeing.

The homes of famous artists, such as the sculptor Carl Milles and the royal painter Prince Eugene, in the Stockholm area, and painters Anders Zorn and Carl Larsson in Dalarna, are now museums. The palatial home of the Hallwyl family in Stockholm gives a fascinating glimpse into the life of a wealthy nineteenth-century industrialist. The works of children's author Astrid Lindgren, world-famous for her character Pippi Longstocking, are immortalized in the delightful *Junibacken* museum in Stockholm.

Check out the theaters in Stockholm, especially the Royal Dramatic Theater (*Dramaten)* and the Culture House (*Kulturhuset*). There is also a local theater in Malmö.

Both Gothenburg and Stockholm have thriving opera seasons. Stockholm has both the traditional Royal Opera and the alternative People's Opera (*Folkoperan*). Heading north, an old quarry in the village of Rättvik has been transformed into a magnificent outdoor arena. Each July and August an outstanding season of concerts and opera is produced *en plein air.*

Stockholm's historic *Konserthus,* site of the Nobel Prize ceremonies, is home to the Royal Philharmonic Orchestra under the talented young American conductor Alan Gilbert. The city's contemporary *Berwaldshallen* concert house is the home of Sweden's Radio Symphony Orchestra.

Government subsidies enable ordinary people to attend quality performances at half the price of New York tickets. Dress can range from elegant to casual, as the typical Swede does not feel obliged to dress up to attend the opera.

POPULAR CULTURE

There is also a thriving rock, jazz, and blues scene. One of the most famous jazz musicians in Sweden is American-born drummer Ronnie Gardiner, who produces a high-quality jazz showcase called "Ronnie's Room" each October and November at Nalen in Stockholm. The Stockholm Jazz Festival each July is also an extremely popular event.

A relatively new phenomenon is the emergence of American-style outdoor festivals and events, and adaptations of the European "carnival." A few noteworthy ones: the *Karnevals* in Lund and in Stockholm, the latter in May every three years under the name *Quarneval,* and the "Gay Pride Parade" in Stockholm each August. (Check out the European section of the International Festivals and Events Association Web site at www.ifeaeurope.com for dates and locations.)

THE GREAT OUTDOORS

Nature provides most Swedes with endless leisure-time opportunities. Hiking, walks in the woods, berry picking, and picnicking are all favorite pastimes. In national parks in the far north, such as Sarek, the Swedish Tourist Foundation maintains trailside huts where hikers can stay for a nominal fee.

By law, "everyman's right" allows the Swedes nearly unlimited access to any land or waterfront area, whether for searching for mushrooms in the spring and fall, or for boating among the 25,000 islands in the Swedish archipelago. The Göta Canal between Gothenburg on the west coast and Stockholm on the east coast is also a popular summer trip for powerboaters. Sweden is also a fisherman's paradise, with over 96,000 lakes and a national border that is mainly coastline. Hunters need to exercise caution, as there are specific seasons for hunting specific species. Additionally, hunters must own or lease land with hunting rights, and a gun permit, issued by the police, is mandatory.

Many towns maintain trails for cross-country skiing, jogging, walking, running, bicycling, and horseback riding. The Swedes are inseparable from nature. It brings them an inner peace and harmony, and is considered by many to be the "new" religion of the Third Millennium.

chapter seven

GETTING AROUND

If you thought California was a big state, then Sweden will seem even more daunting. Running 978 miles (1,574 kilometers) from north to south, it is such a long country that it takes days to drive. As an alternative to road travel, there are domestic flights with SAS, Skyways, and Malmöaviation, with discounts for young people.

Sweden's three principal cities are in the lower one-third of the country. Highways are well maintained, even in wintertime, but the countryside is quite rural, often with gravel roads the further north you go.

The new Öresund toll bridge that opened in 2000 now connects Malmö, at the southern tip of Sweden, to Copenhagen, Denmark, and continental Europe.

TRAINS, BUSES, AND THE SUBWAY

Sweden has an excellent, but expensive, train system, and the major cities such as Stockholm and Gothenburg have well-developed public bus networks, as well as tram (streetcar) services.

Stockholm is the only city in Sweden to have a subway, but unlike other subway systems, most connections from one line to the next take place in the central terminal. Stockholm also has a very good commuter train that services the suburbs from the city center, and a new, high-speed train from Arlanda Airport to the central railway station.

Within Sweden, most long-distance train travel is on the state-owned *Statens Järnvägar* (SJ) rail system, which runs regional, intercity, and express trains. The privately owned Connex runs the northern rail routes and the Stockholm area trains. Special rates are available according to frequency of travel and the time and destination within Sweden, and the staff is friendly and helpful, with an excellent command of English.

Motor coaches or buses connect many of the smaller towns and villages, and are usually cheaper than trains.

The most economical way to travel on Stockholm's subway, commuter trains, or buses is to pre-purchase a travel card for one day, three days, or one month. You can also buy a strip of twenty discounted coupons, called *rabatt kuponger*, which cost SEK 145 for twenty coupons. Within the city center, you may travel as much as you want during a one-hour period for the cost of two coupons.

Tourists can also buy special cards (called the Stockholm Card/*Stockholmskortet*, the Malmö Card/*Malmöskortet*, or the Gothenburg Card/*Göteborgskortet*), which give free admission to museums and attractions, as well as free travel on local buses, the subway, and local trains, and free parking at official city parking lots for a limited period of time.

BOATS

Because so much of Sweden is surrounded by water, ferries and cruise ships also provide transportation to mainland Europe, Russia, and the Baltic States. Stockholm is built on fourteen islands. Its ferry system services two inner-city destinations, as well as certain islands in the Swedish archipelago. Both Silja Line and Viking Line run huge, overnight cruise ship ferries from Stockholm to Finland (about fifteen hours). EstLine has a daily service from Stockholm to the Baltic state of Estonia.

There are commuter car ferries from Helsingborg in southern Sweden to Copenhagen, Denmark; from Gothenburg on the west coast to either Fredrikshavn in Denmark, or to Kiel, Germany; and an overnight car ferry from Gothenburg to Newcastle, England, a crossing that takes about twenty-seven hours, with an hour-stop in Norway. From Germany, the fastest way to southern Sweden is via the catamaran ferry from Rostock to Trelleborg.

ROAD SENSE

Traveling by car in Sweden is not recommended if you have time constraints because the country is so vast. Swedish highways, all toll-free, may have three lanes—one lane each for opposing traffic, and a middle lane for whoever wishes to pass. Some of the larger "super" highways have four lanes. Secondary highways may have only one lane each way, with no apparent passing lane. Slower cars being overtaken must pull over to the side of the road (the "shoulder" or the "breakdown lane" in America) in order to enable a faster car to pass. The first time this happens, an unsuspecting foreigner can have a minor panic attack, thinking a crash or breakdown is imminent.

SPEED LIMITS

Major Highways: 68 miles per hour (110 km/h); between mid-June and mid-August, reduced to 56 miles per hour (90 km/h)

Secondary Highways: 56 miles per hour (90 km/h)

Built-up Areas: 31–43 miles per hour (50–70 km/h)

Near Schools: 19 miles per hour (30 km/h)

N.B.: These speed limits are strictly enforced.

Getting Caught

Getting caught in Sweden is, in a word, expensive. A fine or prison sentence is the typical punishment for reckless driving. For driving without a license, you may be sentenced to a fine or a maximum of six months in jail. If you are stopped for speeding, the police may confiscate your license on the spot. The normal penalty for speeding is a fine, which is indexed-linked to income. Whether or not you get your license back is up to the county court. The owner of the vehicle is responsible for parking fines, and these, too, are steep.

Drinking and Driving

The drunk-driving laws are among the strictest in Europe, with the maximum blood alcohol limit set at 0.2 per mil (0.02 percent). For most drivers, this means a maximum consumption of just one alcoholic drink. In practice, it means drivers cannot drink and drive. Roadblocks and random Breathalyzer tests are legal. Fines are *extremely* heavy, and imprisonment is a possibility.

Driver's Licenses

Visitors to Sweden from outside the EU may use their own driver's license for up to one year, after which they have to obtain a Swedish license. Sweden has reciprocal agreements with other

DRIVING TIPS PARTICULAR TO SWEDEN

- The use of seat belts is mandatory for drivers and front-seat passengers, and children, by law, must ride in the backseat.

- There is no free parking in Stockholm except between 5:00 p.m. and 9:00 a.m. and on weekends. To get a parking coupon for your dashboard, put money in one of the hungry dispensing boxes located along the sidewalk, and purchase the amount of time you require. Parking fines are exceedingly expensive—starting at SEK 400 and upward to SEK 700!

- Hydroplaning can occur in slush, as well as on wet road surfaces.

- Black ice forms in the wintertime on shady stretches of road that tend to be colder than others. If you go into a skid, steer in the direction of the skid and avoid using your brakes.

- When parking overnight in the wintertime, pull your windshield wiper blades out at right angles from the windshield to keep them from freezing onto the windshield.

- Beware of elk and reindeer, especially in May, June, September, and October. Dawn and dusk are the most dangerous times, because of low visibility, and animals caught in the headlights of a car tend to freeze. Up north, where the snow is very deep, it is not at all uncommon to see entire families of reindeer walking along the roadway.

  Tip: If you should hit a cloven-hoofed animal, it is mandatory to report the accident to the police.

EU countries accepting their drivers' licenses, but not with the United States. Some corporations arrange for special, temporary Swedish driving permits, good for one year at a time, for foreign workers they bring into Sweden on a limited assignment basis. Most Swedes attend a driving school, and the lessons are extremely expensive. Young Swedes tend to get their driver's licenses at a later age than their counterparts in America.

Although the written test for a Swedish driver's license is available in English, few foreigners pass this on the first attempt. There is also a road test, including a test of driving on ice. There is a fee for each repeat test.

If you are just on a short visit to Sweden, this will not be a concern. Otherwise, it could be prudent to investigate obtaining a driver's license in another EU country to take advantage of reciprocal arrangements with Sweden. A third way of coping with the high failure rate is to take your road test in the most rural Swedish community you can find, so as to minimize distractions.

Jaywalking

The Swedes frown on jaywalking. However, the influx of immigrants to Sweden, coupled with increased travel abroad, has caused many Swedes to take a more relaxed view of things.

It is compulsory for drivers to stop for

pedestrians in the crosswalk or when they are stepping from the curb to cross the street, whether or not there is a traffic light. Failure to do so will result in a stiff fine.

LOCAL TRANSPORTATION

The sophistication of the local transportation systems depends on the population size of the area. Stockholm (east coast), Gothenburg (west coast), and Malmö (south) all have well-developed bus and train services. Gothenburg and Norrköping have trams (trolley cars); only Stockholm is large enough to have a subway system, and a serious rush hour. There are also numerous bicycle lanes. The best way of exploring the city centers is still by foot.

TAXIS

Hiring a Swedish taxi is like having a private chauffeur. The tip is included in the fare. It is exceedingly easy to book a cab for a small additional fee (approximately SEK 30); otherwise, there are taxi stands in certain parts of the city centers. An available taxi has an illuminated sign on its roof.

Certain companies have an automated booking system linked to the telephone system and can read the address of the phone from which you are dialing. A recording asks you to confirm the order by pushing "1" for "yes." The recording will repeat the confirmation, and—here is the important part—if you don't confirm a second time by pushing "1" again, your booking does not go through. You can also stay on the line, and an operator will speak to you in English if you ask.

Taxis tend to be more expensive in Sweden because of two things: the 25 percent sales tax and the pre-calculated tip. Most cab companies have fixed prices to and from the airport, although these are more expensive going to the airport than from it. Ask before you get in. Beware of "black-market taxis," which not only are unlicensed, but are also known to charge fees equivalent to a ransom.

WHERE TO STAY

Because of supply and demand, as well as the high Swedish sales tax, staying in Sweden is perceived to be expensive. In fact, it does not have to be. Swedish accommodations run the gamut from beautifully located, classic hotels, to very reasonably priced hostels and bed and breakfasts. All have high standards. Between May and November, occupancy rates in Stockholm run at around 80 percent, with the exception of July, when most Swedes disappear into the countryside or out into the archipelago, and all business comes to a standstill. Check out the special offers on travel-related Web sites. Prices quoted will generally include breakfast and sales tax. The central booking agency for hotels and youth hostels in the Stockholm area is *Hotellcentralen*, found at www.stockholmtown.com. For bed and breakfast, go to www.bedbreakfast.a.se. The Swedish Touring Club (STF/IYHF) at www.meravsverige.nu lists hostels in Sweden, some of which are actually floating hostels in beautiful waterfront locations. Some hostels are only open during the summer. Most hotels offer less expensive rates on weekends year-round and daily during the (low) summer season. Credit cards are universally accepted.

"Everyman's right" allows campers the right to erect a tent for one night in the countryside or on an island in the archipelago even if the land is fenced, as long as due respect is shown for the property owners. For stays longer than one night, or for group camping, you should always ask permission from the owner.

Sweden has approximately 750 "formal" campsites, about 200 of which are open year-round. Most operate seasonally from late May to early September. Note that the weather can be very unpredictable. Campsites are inspected and

rated between one and three stars, and officially
authorized campsites have a green sign with a
white "C" superimposed on a black tent. With a
veritable camper's paradise at your fingertips, you
will be able to find many waterfront sites near the
ocean or one of the 96,000 lakes, as well as
campgrounds with such amenities as canoeing,
windsurfing, horseback riding, and tennis.
Approximately 300 sites also rent out cottages, log
cabins, and chalets, where you can get the feeling
of camping without depriving yourself of creature
comforts such as beds. The national parks system
manages a series of trailside huts for dedicated
hikers in the northern mountain ranges.
Contact the Swedish Touring Club (above) for
more details.

Sweden is one of the last remaining unspoiled
wildernesses in the Western world, and its
outdoor life is unparalleled. While hotel

accommodations
can be very simple,
as in the very
northernmost
regions, the
outstandingly
beautiful scenery of woodlands, mountain ranges,
and waterfronts affords the urban-weary
traveler an unrivaled, revitalizing communion
with nature.

HEALTH AND SECURITY

Sweden is one of the safest countries in the world, so the danger (for women especially) is to forget to be as vigilant in a city like Stockholm as you would be in any other large city.

> The emergency number for police, fire, and ambulance is 112, and can be dialed free from any public telephone.

Swedish hospitals are up-to-date, and almost all doctors and caregivers speak English. Most, but not all, Swedish hospitals have an emergency clinic. Your hotel or a taxi driver will know where the closest one is; otherwise, dial 112 and speak in English.

For nonemergency treatment, there are neighborhood clinics called *Vårdcentral*. They reserve a certain number of time slots each day for urgent appointments. In both the doctor's office and the pharmacy, it is important to take a number while waiting.

For dental emergencies, large cities will have an after-hours dentist whose number is listed in the telephone book. The number for telephone directory service in Sweden is 118 118. Dental care in Sweden (for Swedes) is subsidized.

One caution: in general, Swedish doctors do

not take your temperature or blood pressure during a routine office visit. It is useful to know the generic names of any drugs you need or find helpful, so that you can suggest to them what you would like. They will usually oblige.

Foreign visitors from non-EU countries should take out medical insurance in advance of departure to cover treatment by both doctors and hospitals. Those from EU countries may get free medical care in Sweden, but they must produce form E111 and a valid passport or identification card. It is always wise to check with your local insurance company prior to traveling.

Sweden enjoys a state-funded medical service, although some people supplement government coverage with private insurance as the waiting lists can be long for non-life-threatening treatments. Swedish patients pay up to a maximum "ceiling" for doctors' visits, after which all visits are free for the remainder of the year. Medical personnel in Sweden are exceedingly kind and compassionate to foreigners.

Most Americans are shocked to find out that a doctor's visit (for a Swede) is only SEK 140—which is less than US $20—and equally shocked to be greeted by a doctor casually clad in a lab coat and slacks, even wearing sandals with socks. But do not judge him by this.

Prescriptions (*recept*) must be filled in the state-owned pharmacy, called *Apoteket*. Swedish pharmacists are given considerable latitude in prescribing over-the-counter remedies, and there is also a growing practice of homeopathic medicine. As with doctors' fees, there is an equivalent payment ceiling for prescription medicines, roughly US $145 per year per person, after which all prescriptions for the remainder of the year are free. Note: non-EU patients do not have this benefit, but immigrants with either temporary or permanent Swedish residency permits do.

chapter eight

BUSINESS BRIEFING

Sweden has looked to the outside world for business and trade since the days of the Vikings. Sweden's own Industrial Revolution in the 1870s and early 1900s quickly revealed that the available customer base within the country was limited, and that economic prosperity depended on trade relations abroad. In the 1930s, when the newly empowered Social Democrats were attempting to nationalize much of private business, successful Swedish industrialists adopted a survival technique: they simply became invisible, both within Sweden and abroad. The Wallenbergs, one of Sweden's oldest and most successful business families, best express this in their family motto: *Esse non videri*, "To be, not to be seen," borrowed from the Prussian King Friedrich II (1712–86).

Thus, on the one hand, there was industrial reliance on international trade conducted by low-profile, profit-motivated companies, and on the other, personal survival in rural areas (where most people lived until the Second World War) dependent on conformity and cooperation. Just as the Jante Law affected the rural population by discouraging individuality, so it influenced the decision of Swedish capitalists to remain invisible.

Even understanding this background, most English-speakers still find the Swedish way of doing business confusing. Cultural signals such as friendliness, informality, and the use of English lead many to assume that Swedish business style is similar to their own. In fact, it has more in common with the Japanese. Below, we look at some of the culturally specific ways that make doing business with Swedish companies different.

OFFICE ETIQUETTE AND PROTOCOL

Swedish offices are extremely informal by American or British standards. Most have an "open door" policy, ensuring transparency of transactions and easy accessibility, even at the highest levels, by all staff. Since all are equal, everyone is on a first-name basis. Business cards do not necessarily carry a title. Dress is casual and functional, with the predominant color being black. Other than those professions that have a business "uniform," such as lawyers or bankers, most Swedes come to work in slacks or jeans, with casual sweaters or shirts, always open-necked and without ties. Part of this is functional, part economic. Swedish salaries for well-educated employees are low compared with those in competitor countries, although unskilled Swedish employees are relatively well-paid compared to their counterparts elsewhere. The average payroll deductions for taxes are 31 percent, although higher income earners can be taxed up to a maximum of 50 percent. We have seen that the sales tax is also high—25 percent on every purchase except food, which is 12 percent, and medicine, which is not taxed. That means that the purchasing power of the received salary in Sweden is not as strong as it would be in other countries.

Highly educated Swedes form an almost incestuous group due to their post-high school training. Almost all business activity is concentrated geographically in the southern third of the country, in Stockholm, Gothenburg, and, to a much lesser extent, Malmö.

Many successful Swedish businessmen are multilingual, and have studied or worked abroad for at least one year, often in America or England, Germany, or France. They tend to live in the same suburbs, belong to the same clubs, maintain their university-days' friendships, and seek summer vacation homes in the same areas. At the upper levels Swedish business leaders are all interconnected, and

IT'S ABOUT TIME!

The workweek is Monday through Friday from 8:30 or 9:00 a.m. until 5:00 p.m. (which is always written 17:00). You can set your watch by lunch hour (everyone stops at exactly 12 noon) and closing time. There are usually two fifteen-minute coffee breaks, mid-morning and mid-afternoon.

The workweek is thirty-seven to forty hours; overtime is rare, and heavily regulated. Time off due to the illness of employees or their children is generous, as is parental leave at childbirth. Two paid-leave months are mandatory "daddy months." Sweden was the first country in the world to enact this.

Swedish workers, by law, get twenty-five days' (five weeks') paid vacation and twelve paid holidays per year. Many people take all five weeks between midsummer in June through the first week in August—a holdover from the old days when factories closed in July. All workers then vacationed at the same time so that production lines would not be affected. Some legal holidays are contrived to fall on a Monday or Friday. When they fall on a Tuesday or Thursday, the worker may work overtime in order to take a "squeeze day" (*klämdag*) to create a four-day break.

Get the Timing Right

If you are negotiating a contract or conducting business that is time-sensitive, beware of the solstices in Sweden. Spring or summer contracts should be finalized by March if possible, as there are some years when there are only two full five-day working weeks between Easter and August, and after Lucia Day on December 13 most business comes to a standstill until after Sweden's "third" Christmas on January 13.

Appointments are made in advance, and punctuality is extremely important. If there is any status symbol at all, it is how far in advance a person's schedule is booked. It is generally not difficult to get an appointment with a high-level person, but it is difficult to "read" the various spoken and body-language signs. To American or British people often the visual cultural cues will seem to be similar to their own, but the real test of communication is whether these are interpreted correctly.

Nonconfrontation in Action

John, an American executive living in Sweden, was talking to a Swede with whom he hoped to do business. The Swede was friendly, and very interested in John's business idea. His English was good. He asked John to leave his materials with him, and said he would like to talk again in a couple of weeks. Two weeks later John made a follow-up call, and left a message as the man was unavailable. He called again, and again. Knowing patience was a Swedish virtue, he waited. Six weeks later, he tried again, with the same result.

What is the Swedish interpretation of this? One Swede suggested that circumstances had changed in two weeks, or that the man had never had the authority to approve such a project in the first place. Or perhaps his English was not as good as John had thought. To discuss any of this with John would have meant a loss of face. Another suggested that he was unable to get consensus to move forward. Why not take the phone call? Obviously, it had made the Swede uncomfortable, he felt it might have involved confrontation, and he chose to ignore the situation. It would then simply cease to exist.

THE COFFEE CULTURE

Coffee plays an extremely important role in keeping the office running smoothly. There is a coffee break at 3:00 p.m. each day, during which it is considered rude to continue working. (Your colleagues will feel that you are trying to outshine them and put pressure on them by doing more than they do; it also makes you stand out, which is very anti-Jante.) Everyone partakes of the daily coffee break (*fika*), even the boss, since according to the Jante Law, he is no better than anyone else. (In fact, he or she may even make the coffee for others!) In some offices, there is also a coffee break in the morning, around 9:30 to 10:00 a.m. If an office celebrates a colleague's birthday, it is during the coffee break. The birthday celebrant is expected to provide the refreshments—usually a special type of pistachio-green marzipan-covered cake (called a princess cake, or *princesstårta*) layered with whipped cream, vanilla pudding, and raspberry jam filling.

BUSINESS ENTERTAINING

Believing firmly in the separation of business and home life, the Swedes rarely entertain business colleagues in their homes. Swedish businessmen may not drink excessively within Sweden, but they have an honestly earned reputation for boisterous and enthusiastic consumption once out of their own country.

MOBILE PHONES

Sweden is one of the most "wired" countries in the world. Subscriptions are inexpensive. With the advent of dual-band mobile phones, Swedish businessmen are accessible at all times, and the Swedish business culture expects them to be so. Do not be surprised to be interrupted by a mobile phone ringing during your business meeting with a Swede. Think of it as a knock on the door. The Swede will usually handle the situation politely.

MANAGEMENT STYLES

The Swedish organizational model is flat and nonhierarchal, with responsibilities decentralized. Status and title play little role in Swedish business life; personal responsibility does. Management focuses on shared visions and values, and a sense of closeness between management and employees. Swedish employees are not afraid of being openly honest with their bosses.

Discussions, in the Swedish style, show no extremes of emotion; factual presentations, unembellished and direct, are valued over flowery language and rhetorical buildup. Where Americans expect—and give—a lot of praise, Swedish managers are sparing. Swedes do not give, nor are they comfortable receiving, praise for doing what they were supposed to do anyway.

It singles them out and makes them feel apart from the group, which is very anti-Jante. It also makes them aware that they have a boss, whereas they would like to think that all are equal.

Although they take pride in producing quality products, most Swedes have been raised in a noncompetitive environment. They believe a product should stand on its own merits. While Americans will put the full weight of a marketing campaign behind a product launch, the Swedish manager may miss the competitive advantage overseas because he feels his product is better and that time, not marketing, will tell.

The Swedes will work diligently within the time frame allotted, but if a deadline comes up, they may not feel compelled to work overtime if they feel they have been working hard all along, and management may be reluctant to ask for overtime. Commitment to a balanced home life is more important than staying overtime. Service is not a strong concept within the Swedish business sector. Good service or bad, you will not lose your job, nor will you personally earn any more money.

WOMEN IN MANAGEMENT

Under Swedish law, women have equal rights with men. They cannot be discriminated against when it comes to employment, voting, education, and health benefits. Swedish labor laws protect pregnant women, ensuring not only medical leave, but also job reinstatement after maternity leave.

In 2003, 53 percent of Members of Parliament were women, which was a world record. The desire to improve the position of women in society has been a major platform in the expansion of the Swedish welfare state, especially in the areas of elder care and child care. As a result, Sweden today has a higher percentage of working-age women in paid jobs than any other nation—74 percent, compared to 79 percent among men—although many of these women work only part-time. Forty-three percent of business management graduates and 21 percent of engineering graduates are women.

In practice, although Swedish women represent 53 percent of the workforce, only 2 percent of the chief executive officers, 5 percent of the board members, and 8 percent of the members of higher corporate management are women. In short, men hold the majority of top-level executive positions. A salary distribution study of occupational groups requiring higher education, undertaken by Statistics Sweden in 1998, showed that men earned more than women in every category surveyed.

Foreign female executives will not find that they must establish their seniority with Swedish men, who are accustomed to equality. However, this is not necessarily true of foreign businessmen in Sweden. It is, therefore, advisable for women to have their titles printed on their business cards.

Dress for female executives in Sweden is similar to that of a female lawyer: conservative, usually dark colors, such as black, brown, or gray, with simple jewelry. Dress for office workers such as secretaries is casual. If you, as a woman, look too good, too rich, or too sexy, you will be the target for the "royal Swedish envy," described earlier.

Independence and a sense of equality are so strongly cultivated and valued in Swedish women that many shun the traditional male courtesies of opening doors or lending a helping hand—and younger Swedish men are gradually learning not to offer! American businesswomen may therefore be shocked when the Swedish man lets the door swing back in her face or doesn't offer to help her with her coat. She should recognize the backward compliment that she is being treated as an equal.

LEADERSHIP AND DECISION-MAKING

In Swedish offices decisions are made consensually by a leadership group. The role of the Swedish boss in decision-making meetings is to ensure that various viewpoints are aired, and to sum up the group consensus, so that all leave knowing what has been agreed upon. It takes great skill to move things forward in this fashion. To an outsider unaccustomed to consensus, the final product appears to be a watered-down version of the original. The process can be laborious, and a company in a more time-oriented country can lose its competitive edge. To a Swede, it is vitally important that all agree on the final decision, no matter how long it takes. The manager's role is to make this happen.

Generally, once consensus has been achieved, each Swedish participant knows his role in carrying out the decision; most Americans, on the other hand, want it spelled out.

PRESENTATION AND LISTENING STYLES
Swedish presentation style can border on minimalism. The Swedes will get to the point immediately without a lot of "hype" or buildup. Facts are valued; glitz is not. The Swedish language has fewer words than English. Thus, with their economical style of writing and speaking, they can come across to an English-speaker as being a bit abrupt and cold. They will also avoid confrontational language. A Swede will err on the side of promising too little rather than

promising too much, as some Americans are wont to do. He mistrusts the American tendency toward exaggeration.

In a meeting, the Swede will patiently wait for his turn to speak. He is a polite listener and will not interrupt a presentation. His questioning style will not be loud or angrily argumentative, and he will strive for harmony among those present.

NEGOTIATION STYLES

Swedish meetings follow an agenda, but *Roberts' Rules of Order*, so favored by American boardrooms, is not used as the protocol roadmap. Meetings start and end exactly on time. Extraneous chitchat and joking are frowned upon. Although top-level executives may lead the negotiations, generally middle management will participate in the detailed discussions. Although each member of the Swedish team may have a different field of expertise, in general, all will have to agree before the deal can go forward. It is important for the presenter to remember to direct his presentation to the team, not the individual, even though the final decision may be made by the CEO based on the recommendations of the negotiating team.

Whereas American negotiators generally start with a high asking price and expect to negotiate downward, Swedes start with a realistic asking price and may resent attempts to be talked down from what they consider to be a fair first offer—unless, of course, the proposed reduction can be backed up factually. The Swede does not see it as a win/lose situation, but rather as a win/win situation whereby each party should be satisfied with the outcome.

Verbal agreements are considered binding in Sweden, although they are usually written up subsequently as contracts. Swedish law, especially purchase and contract law, covers most possible situations. A Swedish contract, therefore, does not have to be as specific as an Anglo-Saxon contract. However, according to one Swedish CEO, Swedish lawyers do not have a strong foundation in business and economics, so today the Anglo-Saxon approach to drafting contracts, whereby each hypothetical situation is addressed, has gained currency. It would be unusual and unnecessary for a Swedish company to bring in a lawyer at the initial discussion phase of the contract negotiation.

WORKING IN SWEDEN

Non-Swedes who are not part of the Shengen Agreement of the EU need a work visa, obtainable from the immigration department.

All employees in Sweden have a work contract. Verbal employment contracts are legally binding, although most people also receive a written contract within a month of employment. Three to six months' notice of termination is required of either party; the amount of advance notice varies according to length of time employed and stature of the employee's position on the organizational chart. If the employer wishes to terminate a permanent contract, he usually will have to buy out the remainder of the contract, in which case advance notice is irrelevant—the employee will be paid anyway. Employees fall into one of two categories:

- **Temporary contract (*Tidsbegränsad anställning*)** Maximum duration is 650 hours over six months. At the end of that time, the employer must either let the employee go or convert him to permanent status. The trial contract cannot be renewed for the same person to continue in the same job.
- **Permanent contract (*Tillsvidareanställning*)** The worker may not be dismissed, demoted, or laid off unless there is just cause.

STARTING A BUSINESS IN SWEDEN

If you are not a Swedish national, you must first have a valid residency permit and a work visa in order to start your own business in Sweden. These are obtainable from the immigration authorities. See www.migrationsverket.se for information in English. There are some very strict conditions that must be fulfilled before you will be granted a residency and work permit (should your business fail, the state does not want to be responsible for supporting an alien with its wide and very expensive safety net of benefits). You will have to submit a detailed, written business plan that has been reviewed and certified by independent Swedish auditors (whom you have paid). You will also have to show proof of financial solvency during the start-up period.

A Tip for Entrepreneurs

It can be more advantageous strategically to form a relationship with a reputable Swedish company than to bid for a contract as an outsider. There is still a bias toward giving contracts to Swedish companies rather than foreign-owned ones, no matter the level of competency.

All businesses, even simple proprietor consultancies, must register with both the Patent and Registration Office (*Patent och Registeringsverket*, or PRV) and the sales tax (*moms,* the Swedish equivalent of valued-added tax, or VAT) authorities. Note: one of the unexpected cash-flow drains on new Swedish businesses is sales tax payments based on *estimated* income.

TWO EXCELLENT RESOURCES

The Invest in Sweden Agency (ISA) Web site at www.isa.se is a wealth of information for anyone contemplating starting a business in Sweden. It includes an up-to-date overview of all major costs needed to develop a business plan, such as personnel (salaries and benefits), recruitment, accounting, rental of premises and equipment, utilities, insurance, bank services, and car leasing. It also lists financial incentives in Sweden, such as national grants, loans, and credit guarantees.

American companies desiring to set up a Swedish branch will find the U.S. Embassy's Commercial Department in Stockholm an excellent resource, as well.

At 28 percent, corporate taxes on profits in Sweden (versus 38 percent in Germany, 40 percent in the United States, and 42 percent in Japan) are competitive with those in other parts of the world. It is, however, more difficult to make a profit in Sweden. The differentiating factor comes from the high social costs secured by unions for employees. The average Swedish employee costs his Swedish employer an additional 48.52 percent of his base salary in social costs, insurance, and vacation benefits, compared to an average 24.55 percent in costs for an American employee in America. This high social cost is one of the greatest cultural shocks an American businessman can experience.

Statistics from the Organization for Economic Cooperation and Development (OECD) list taxes in Sweden at 52 percent of the gross domestic product, compared to around 45 percent in France, 37 percent in Great Britain, and 29 percent in the U.S.A.

UNIONS

Many foreigners underestimate the power of Swedish labor unions, which count the majority of employees among their membership. Historically, the unions are the reason that Sweden is called a "worker's paradise." Employees cannot be fired or demoted without just cause. Job descriptions cannot be changed without consultation with the relevant union, and a 1977 law ensures that unions participate in decision-making. Union personnel are also present at interviews with prospective employees. Swedish legislation entitles the unions to representation on the boards of directors of companies listed on the stock exchange, and all companies with more than five employees must have a health and safety representative.

It has become so difficult to lay off or dismiss an employee that more employers are turning to temporary "project work" contracts that allow greater flexibility to respond to market or seasonal demands. Other companies may ask their employees to accept a voluntary work reduction, such as from five days a week to four, for a temporary period to get through a bad economic cycle. While the unions did much to alter the deplorable working conditions of the early stages of the Industrial Revolution in Sweden, today they are so powerful that they have a stranglehold on the economic life of the country. Swedish companies are struggling to remain competitive in a market driven by globalization, and many manufacturing companies are looking to Eastern Europe and the Baltic States as a solution to high labor costs.

TEAMWORK

Anglophones and Swedes come to the workplace with two different mindsets. The Swede has grown up in a noncompetitive environment that values teamwork. The greatest security and strength comes from being part of a team that is following a plan that all have agreed upon.

Swedish workers tend to be more independent and autonomous than their American counterparts. Unlike Americans, they are never afraid of their bosses, and they are not in awe of formal titles. A Swedish manager assumes that those on his team are qualified to carry out their assignments, and his role is to coach, not supervise. As opposed to the hierarchical attitudes implicit in the American management style, the Swedish message is that all are equal, even if one happens to be labeled the boss. This attitude is reinforced by the salary structure: the difference in salaries between the American boss and his employees can be quite large; the Swedish differential will not be so great. The Swede is not motivated by salary raises and promotions; the American, who sees these as prestige-building rewards for his personal effort, is.

When beginning a team project, the Swedes will invest group time in mapping out the steps to be followed and who will do what; the Americans will usually assign tasks and leave each individual to figure out his own approach. Americans will take their work home with them, or at least to the neighborhood pub, where the discussions can continue. The Swede will stop working when the big hand is on the twelve, and leave the problem at the office.

MANAGING DISAGREEMENT

Because nearly every Swedish employee is represented by a union, in the case of disagreements reconciliation between employer and employee invariably involves a union representative. It is extremely difficult to fire an individual. There are procedures that must be followed, and the employee is entitled to appeal, via his union representative, in a labor court. It is often easier for the dissatisfied Swedish employer to buy out the remaining contract of the employee. Labor disputes, however, are rare in Sweden; according to the Institute of Management Development, Sweden lost only 3.4 working days per 1,000 inhabitants in 1999–2001 as a result of labor disputes, compared to 28.5 working days lost in the United States and 37.6 in Ireland.

As Sweden interacts increasingly with the world outside Scandinavia, new attitudes and lifestyles are affecting the workplace. The rising importance of the Internet, increased travel and work experience overseas, and the cumulative effect of immigrants assimilating into Swedish life have all made an impact. Corporate mergers and acquisitions also introduce their share of different managerial styles, giving rise to intercultural management specialists who can help smooth the waters. The trend of the 1970s for international companies to send their own managers to Sweden on long-term assignments has been replaced by short-term assignments with a handover to local Swedish management. They have found that the most effective way of operating in Sweden is to have local managers running their subsidiaries.

chapter nine

COMMUNICATING

LANGUAGE

One of the marvelous things about visiting
Sweden is that everyone under the age of about
sixty can speak English. English-language courses
have been mandatory for over fifty years in
Swedish schools. French and German are popular
third languages. As with any language, the degree
of fluency depends on its use by the speaker. A
brand of English and a type of humor that Swedes
jokingly call "Swenglish" (*Svengelska*) has
emerged, where the two languages are playfully
mixed to create texture in a conversation.

A branch of the Indo-European family of
languages, Swedish is Teutonic in origin.
Norwegians, Danes, and Swedes can more or less
understand each other. Although the Finns speak
a language distantly related to Hungarian, about
6 percent of Finns are Swede-Finns, stemming
from the years when Finland belonged to Sweden,
and Swedish is taught as a mandatory second
language in Finnish schools. Visitors speaking
Dutch, Afrikaans, or German, as well as English,

generally learn Swedish much more quickly than those with other languages as their native tongue.

Swedish has a smaller vocabulary than English, so when a Swede speaks English in a literal fashion he may seem abrupt. The Swedish style of speaking and writing is very economical.

TV AND RADIO

The Swedish television stations are SVT1 and SVT2, both state-run public service channels; and TV3, TV4, and Channel 5. Cable TV offers CNN, Sky News, BBC, MTV, Eurosport, and TV1000, a movie channel, as well as broadcasts from various French, German, Norwegian, Finnish, and Danish channels. Most apartment buildings are wired for cable, and many are now wired for broadband.

If you are relocating to Sweden, it is easier to buy a television there than to try to adapt an American or British model. American NTSC-recorded videos will not play in Swedish PAL VCRs, nor will American VCRs record PAL-broadcast programs. As for the content, nudity on television and in film is considered natural; violence is not condoned. Both are shown.

There are a number of radio stations with a wide range of offerings. P6, Stockholm

International, offers English-language programs on 89.6 MHz.

MAKING CONTACT

As more and more Swedish businessmen interact with Americans, the need for a formal letter of introduction has become less common, although it is still appreciated.

Appointments, however, should be made well in advance, preceded by a typewritten, introductory letter. Sweden is an extremely orderly country, and appointment books fill up weeks and months in advance. It is not difficult to get to talk with a high-level executive, although, as we have seen, it may be difficult to interpret the response. It is courteous to write a follow-up letter thanking the executive for the meeting. Do not initially communicate by e-mail or fax if you do not know the recipient.

Job applications should be brief and typed. They can be written in English, but applications in Swedish may make a better impression. The downside to the latter is that the response from the prospective employer may also be in Swedish. Often, proficiency certificates (similar to diplomas) are required. If you are studying Swedish, or already have a residency permit (as a non-EU alien), it is helpful to mention this.

TELEPHONES

The Swedes place a high value on staying connected. Most Swedish homes have telephones, and almost every Swede old enough to dial a telephone number has a cell phone.

The country code for Sweden is 46, followed by a city code and the telephone number. The toll-free number for emergencies is 112, and it can be used for police, fire, or ambulance services. The operators speak English. There is a time-based fee for talking to the operator.

The yellow pages (*gula sidorna*) list businesses by type, the white pages are residential listings, and the pink pages are business numbers arranged alphabetically by company name. Remember that the Swedish alphabet has three additional letters: Ä, Å, and Ö. These come at the end of the alphabet in the order listed. In Europe, "de" or "von" are considered to be embellishments leading up to the last (family) name, and it is under the latter that you will find the listing. Thus, the Swede will look for de Witt to be filed under "W," whereas the American will look under "D." Swedish telephone books (referred to as "catalogues") include detailed, cross-indexed street maps.

Foreigners may find Swedish telephone phone numbers confusing. The numbers following a city code can be of varying length. To telephone long-distance within Sweden, dial 0 followed by the city code, and the telephone number. Thus, a Stockholmer would dial 031 to call Gothenburg, but he would not dial the Stockholm city code 08 to dial a number within Stockholm. To dial outside Sweden, dial 00 before the country code.

MAJOR CITY CODES	
Stockholm (0)8	Gothenburg (0)31
Malmö (0)40	Uppsala (0)18

Swedish mobile telephone numbers, when dialed within Sweden, start with 073, 070, 0706, or a host of others depending upon the telephone service provider. When calling any fixed (as opposed to mobile) city number in Sweden from a Swedish mobile phone, you must dial 0 plus the city code even if you are calling next door.

It is best to research your mobile service before leaving home, as each subscription varies, and American mobile phones do not work in Europe unless they are tri-band, meaning that they can be converted to the European GSM system.

Sweden is the Silicon Valley of Scandinavia, and it is easy to buy the most up-to-date mobile phone quite inexpensively when you combine the purchase with a subscription to a mobile phone service—but, as with many other transactions, you must have a Swedish personal number (*personnummer*) in order to subscribe.

Because mobile phones are so common in Sweden, there are few public telephone pay booths. The ones that still exist take disposable plastic "cash cards," which can be purchased from convenience stores and newsdealers, or cash. A few take credit cards. You cannot place a collect call within Sweden, but you can call collect overseas through your home number.

USEFUL NUMBERS

Collect Overseas: Call 020-79 + country code + number

Overseas: Call 00* + country code + number (Note: some people subscribe to a discounted long-distance service and may therefore dial an access number other than 00.)

Directory Assistance (National): 118 118 (There is a time-based fee for talking to the operator. Operators speak English.)

Directory Assistance (International): 118 119 (There is a time-based fee for talking to the operator. Operators speak English.)

Avoid using a hotel phone if you can—hotel surcharges can be horrendous. If you must do so, use a telephone credit card if possible.

Swedes usually answer the phone with their name or phone number. When finishing a call, they will say, "*Hej,*" "*Hej då,*" or even "*Hej, hej.*" They do not call later than 10:00 p.m.

For those needing to connect to the Internet, the larger cities of Stockholm and Gothenburg have Internet cafés, and most major hotels have Internet connections and business centers, but the latter can be quite modest by U.S. standards, and may have limited hours and/or access.

POST

The Swedish postal system (*Posten*) is very efficient and very expensive. It operates on a for-profit basis. There is one mail delivery per day during the week, and no weekend delivery service. Swedish addresses contain a postal code that expedites mail delivery. Tenants subletting from another tenant must add their name under the nameplate on the door, and mail addressed to them should have their name "care of" the firsthand tenant.

In addition to the sale of stamps and mail delivery, the post office offers banking services that include receiving direct-deposits from employers and paying bills via a type of checking account called a *postgirot* account. You can also have mail forwarded (very expensive) and collect parcels at the "will call" desk. Be wary of receiving packages from overseas in excess of US $50 (£28), as the Swedish tax authorities will be waiting with outstretched hands. If you do not want to pay the duty, the post office will return the parcel to the sender at no extra cost to either you or the sender. You can then make alternative arrangements with the sender.

Post office hours are from 10:00 a.m. to 6:00 p.m. weekdays, and 10:00 a.m. to 1:00 p.m. on Saturdays. Today many post offices are closed, and the service is handled by the Swedish kiosk chain Pressbyrån, or some supermarkets and gas stations. You will find mailboxes in two colors: blue for local post and yellow for national and international post. At Christmastime, special red mailboxes for Christmas cards appear in the cities. Postage for Christmas cards is reduced for a certain period before and after Christmas (usually ending January 7). Postage costs are based on first-class ("A" Post) and second-class ("B" Post) rates, differentiated by the priority given to the delivery. Postage to the other Nordic countries (Finland, Norway, Denmark) is less expensive than to the rest of the world. The price includes the 25 percent sales tax (VAT/*moms*). The post office's Web site is www.posten.se.

Alternative delivery systems include DHL and UPS. Federal Express delivers to Sweden, but is not commonly used for sending items out of the country. There is no such thing as overnight service to America. A two-day service can cost as much as US $70/£38 for a letter.

E-MAIL

Because snail mail, telephoning, and fax transmissions are expensive, most Swedes communicate via e-mail. Do not be put off, however, if the response is not immediate. Anyone using a second language wants to write and spell that language properly . . . or not write at all.

COMMUNICATION STYLES

The Swede, with his economical way of expressing himself, values directness and brevity. He focuses on content, rather than relationship. However, with growing internationalism, Swedes are becoming increasingly influenced by the American style of openness and warmth.

People will not necessarily interrupt their conversation to introduce a new arrival at their group—something to which a foreigner might take offense. They may also continue speaking in Swedish, being more efficient for their immediate purpose, rather than switching to English for the benefit of an English speaker. There is no personal affront intended, but rather expediency. This is less likely to happen with younger people.

Seriousness and Humor

Swedish humor can be understated and quite dry. In business situations, humor is rarely used; privately, Swedes use the verbal economy of a poet to make precisely the right humorous remark. Where Americans use humor in public to bridge awkward situations, Swedes would either avoid the awkward situation in the first place, or plunge directly in, meeting it head on, but at the same time leaving as few ripples as possible because of their impersonal, nonconfrontational style.

COOPERATION

The Swedes learn from an early age to work together to solve problems. In school, they are placed in teams to tackle an assignment and arrive at a group analysis. The strongest are taught to help the weakest. The leader is the spokesperson for all, but no one is a follower because all have arrived at the solution or analysis together. Honesty and forthrightness are valued traits.

HONOR

Another aspect of Swedish communication is the value placed on an individual's word. In short, verbal agreements are morally and legally binding, so Swedes are both careful and parsimonious with words. On an informal basis, for example, Swedes hear "Let's do lunch" as a commitment to get together, much the same way as they interpret the omnipresent American expression, "Have a nice day," as a flattering and sincere expression of sentiment.

The Swedes are modest in their own assessment of personal success, and react negatively to hyperbole. America is a competitive society, and anyone who is overly modest gets nowhere. In Sweden, anyone who is not modest is immediately suspect. It is a fine line.

CONVERSATION

Practical, orderly, and efficient, the conversational style in Sweden mirrors its lifestyle. The Swedish language is very direct. Some would even call it blunt. Traditionally, and particularly in the north, Swedes are uncomfortable with small talk in casual conversation, preferring silence to nonsense; and they are equally uncomfortable with confrontation, going to great lengths to avoid open disagreement.

Swedes participating in group meetings will not often ask questions after a presentation; they will wait until the group disperses and then ask questions directly of the presenter. Partly this is because they do not want to be embarrassed; partly, they do not want to draw attention to themselves. (The Jante Law lives on.) Outside a business context, however, they can be charming, funny, friendly, and witty, and most go out of their way to make foreigners feel welcome.

Consider striving for a balance when talking with a Swede, avoiding asking prying questions, and letting him gradually feel his way into offering details a little at a time. Americans will find this a major stylistic difference in conversation, but the Swedes will appreciate it. You will feel warmly rewarded when you do finally get to meet the "real" Swede lurking behind all the formal armor. Swedes are charming and gracious hosts, and it is an honor to be allowed into their private lives.

BODY LANGUAGE

The Swedes use little body language in communication, preferring a calm, economically spoken sentence to effusive gesticulation. Given the national penchant for modesty and their strong desire to avoid attracting attention, they speak with little visual "affect" or volume, relying on the words themselves, few as they may be, to carry the message. This "poker face" can be off-putting to English-speakers, who, at the least, expect some sort of smile or warmth during conversation.

One trait particular to Swedes is prolonged direct eye contact while talking or listening. It can be unnerving to the unaccustomed, whereas from the Swedish perspective it shows respect through absolute attentiveness. A Swede may nod his head while listening, but it does not mean that he agrees with what is being said.

CONCLUSION

The CEO of a Swedish investment agency once said the only thing more American than the United States was Sweden, and, on the surface, this seems to be true. Younger Swedes have readily adopted American expressions, style of dress, and entrepreneurial spirit—but underneath it all, they are still Swedes at heart. The skillful cross-cultural traveler knows enough to appreciate the genuine differences and rise to the challenge of adapting to different ways of communicating. A little time patiently invested will yield lasting friendships based on the old-fashioned values of honesty, sincerity, and trust.

Further Reading

Anderson, Bengt. *Swedishness*. Stockholm: Positiva Sverige, 1993, 1995/ Sandberg Trygg, 2000.

Britton, Claes. *Sweden and the Swedes*. Stockholm: The Swedish Institute, 2001.

Downman, Lorna, Paul Britten Austin and Anthony Baird. *Round the Swedish Year. Daily Life and Festivals Through Four Seasons*. Stockholm: The Swedish Institute, 1960.

Hadenius, Stig. *Swedish Politics During the 20th Century*. Stockholm: The Swedish Institute, 1999.

Hagstrom, Jerry. *To Be, Not to be Seen—The Mystery of Swedish Business*. Washington, D.C.: George Washington University School of Business and Public Management, 2001.

Itallie, Nancy van (ed.). *Fodor's 91 Sweden. With Excursions from Stockholm*. New York and London: Fodor's Travel Publications, 1991.

Johnsson, Hans-Ingvar. *Spotlight on Sweden*. Stockholm: The Swedish Institute, 1999.

Liman, Ingemar (transl. Charly Hultén). *Traditional Festivities in Sweden*. Stockholm: The Swedish Institute, 1993.

Moon, Colin. *Sweden: The Secret Files. What They'd Rather Keep to Themselves*. Uppsala, Sweden: Today Press AB/Colin Moon Communications AB, 2002.

Robinowitz, Christina Johansson and Lisa Werner Carr. *Modern-Day Vikings. A Practical Guide to Interacting with the Swedes*. Yarmouth, Maine: Intercultural Press, Inc., 2001.

Rossel, Sven H. and Bo Elbrond-Bek (eds.) (transl. David W. Colbert). *Christmas in Scandinavia*. Lincoln, Nebraska, and London: University of Nebraska, 1999.

Sandell, Kaj. *Eyewitness Travel Guides Stockholm*. London: Dorling Kindersley Ltd., 2001.

Swahn, Jan-Öjvind (transl. Roger Tanner). *Maypoles, Crayfish and Lucia: Swedish Holidays and Traditions*. Värnamo, Sweden: The Swedish Institute, 1997.

A Small Treasury of Swedish Food. Stockholm, Sweden: The Federation of Swedish Farmers (LRF) Information Department, 1987.

Point of Departure. Stockholm Writers Group Anthology. Stockholm: The Stockholm Writers Group, 2003.

Preparing for Your Driving License (Körkortsboken). Sollentuna, Sweden: National Association of Swedish Driving Schools (Sveriges Trafikskolors Riksförbund),1995.

In-Flight Swedish. New York: Living Language, 2001.

Index

accommodation 124–6
Advent 54
alcohol 61, 78, 79–81, 103–6,
    108–9
All Saints. Day 59
American influence 30–31, 35, 50,
    164
Annandag Jul 56
architecture 87
area 10
Ascension Day 58
award ceremonies 64–5

Baltic States 118, 148
banks 100–101
bed and breakfasts 124, 125
Bildt, Carl 23
Blekinge 19
boats 118–19
body language 163–4
boundaries, home 93–4
buses 117, 118
business cards 75, 131
business entertaining 136

campsites 125–6
capital city 10
Carl Philip, Prince 41
Carl XVI Gustaf, King of Sweden
    41, 60
changing lifestyles 97
chivalry 82–3
Christianity 17, 18
Christmas 55–6, 103
cities 26–8
climate 10, 14–16
clothing 73–4, 131–2, 140, 164
clubs 76–7
coffee culture 81, 93, 135–6
communication 70
    styles 160–61
conformity 45
consensus 38–9, 45, 140–41

conversation 162-3
cooperation 161
Copenhagen 27, 116
crayfish parties 61–2
credit cards 101
culture
    high 112–13
    popular 113–14
currency 10
    exchange 101

dating etiquette 72
debit cards 100, 101
decision-making 45, 140–41,
    147–8
Denmark 13, 14, 18, 24, 27, 116
dentist 127
disagreement, managing 150–51
doctors 127–9
drinks 61, 78, 79–81, 103, 104–5,
    108–9
driving 119–23
drunk-driving laws 80–81, 109,
    120

e-mail 160
Easter 57–8
education 92, 95–6
electricity 11, 90
emergency number 127
emigration 22, 30, 48, 50
Epiphany 57
equality 36–7, 140
ethnic makeup 10
European Monetary Union (EMU)
    10, 31, 101
European Union (EU) 25, 31, 122,
    128
Eurozone 31, 82
Evangelical Lutheran Church 10,
    25, 69
Everyman's right (*Allemansrätten*)
    42–3, 125

fairness 35–6, 106
family
    family life and routines 92–3
    makeup 10
    occasions 65–8
fermented herring 62
festivals and events 63–8
Finland 18, 21, 28
food 61, 62, 80, 92–3, 98–9, 103,
    105–8, 136

gardening 87, 109
geography 13–14
gifts 78, 81–2
Gothenburg (Göteborg) 14, 27, 85,
    103, 111, 116, 118, 123, 132,
    158
government 11, 28–9
greetings 74–5, 83

health 127–9
Helsingborg 27, 118
history 16–25
holidays 133–4
honor 162
hospitals 127
hotels 124, 125, 126
humor 161

Iceland 28
identity cards 91
immigration 26, 50, 151
Invest in Sweden Agency 146
invitations home 78–81

Jante Law (Jantelagen) 33–5, 48,
    74, 131, 136, 163
jaywalking 122–3

labor laws 41, 139
lagom ("just enough") 32–3, 35
language 10, 38, 50, 51, 75–6,
    152–3, 162
Lappland 110
leadership 140–41

leisure 109–113
Lindh, Anna 25
listening styles 142
living conditions 85–7
Lucia 54–5
Lund 27
Lutheranism 19, 48

Madeleine, Princess 41
making contact 154
Malmö 14, 27, 85, 116, 123, 132
management styles 137–8
marriage 43–4
May Day 60
media 11
Midsummer 60–61
mobile phones 49, 137
monarchy 40
Mora 110

name, official 10
National Day 64
nationalism 49–50
nature 46–7
negotiation styles 142–3
New Year's 59–60
Nobel Prize 21, 26
nonconfrontation 45–6, 96–7,
    135
nonreligious celebrations 59–62
Norrköping 123
Norway 13, 14, 16, 18, 20, 23, 24,
    119
Novgorod 16

office etiquette and protocol 131–3
orderliness 38
Öresund Bridge 13, 27, 116
Oslo 27
outdoor pursuits 71–2, 109–112,
    114–15
outsiders, attitudes toward 50–51

Palme, Olof 25
parenting 36–7, 94-5

Patent and Registration Office
  (PRV) 145
patience 37–8
Poland 21
political parties 28–9
population 10, 12, 23, 26, 41, 85
post 158–60
praise 46
presentation 141–2
pride 46
punctuality 37, 78, 134

quality of life 84–5
queuing 39, 103–4

radio 153–4
recycling 84–5
religion 10, 19, 69
religious festivals 54–9
renting vs. buying 87–90
residency 91–2
restaurants 106–7
royal family 41
Russia 16, 21, 22, 118

Saab 27, 39
safety 127
St. Martin's Day 62
Samis (Lapps) 12, 26, 102
Sandemose, Aksel 33–4
security 38–9, 40
self-sufficiency 36
sexuality 43–4
shaking hands 75
shoe etiquette 94
shopping 98–100
    alcohol purchase 104–5
    open purchase 104
    shopping hours 99–100
    tips for tourists 101–3
    waiting in line 103–4
Silvia, Queen 41
Skane 12, 19
smörgasbord 107–8
snaps 61, 62, 103

solstices 134
sports 110–112
starting a business in Sweden
  144–7
Stockholm 14, 18, 21, 26–7, 84, 85,
  103, 109–112, 116, 117, 118,
  123, 127, 132, 158
Svensson, the "normal" Swede 43
Swedish model 40–41
Swedish year 52–3

taxation 40, 41, 48, 82, 101–2, 105,
  124, 132, 145–6, 147
taxis 123–4
team-building 71
teamwork 148–50
telephone 11, 90, 155–8
theme parks 109–110
tips, tipping 38, 107
toasting ritual 79–80
tourism 51, 110, 118
trains 116–17, 118
trams 117, 123
travelers' checks 101
Trelleborg 119

unemployment 51
unions 147–8
Uppsala 27

verbal agreements 38, 46, 143, 144
Victoria, Crown Princess 41
video/TV 11, 153
Vikings 12, 32–3
Volvo 12, 27, 39

Walpurgis Night 60
welfare state 24, 28
Whitsunday and Whitmonday 59
women in management 138–40
work contracts 144
work ethic 47–8
working in Sweden 143–4
workweek 133